Focus on Grammar

WORKBOOK

A
BASIC
Course for
Reference
and Practice

Volume B

Focus on Grammar

WORKBOOK

A
BASIC
Course for
Reference
and Practice

Samuela Eckstut

Longman

Focus on Grammar: A Basic Course
for Reference and Practice Workbook, Volume B

Addison-Wesley, 10 Bank Street, White Plains, NY 10606

Editorial Director: Joanne Dresner
Development Editor: Joan Saslow
Production Editorial: Lisa A. Hutchins, Helen B. Ambrosio
Text Design: 6 West Design
Cover Design: A Good Thing, Inc.

ISBN 0-201-76498-9

6 7 8 9 10-CRS-99 98 97

Contents

Unit 8 Simple Past Tense   97

Unit 9 Past Tense of *Be*   114

Unit 10 Nouns and Quantifiers; Modals: *Can, Could, Would*   127

Unit 11 Future; Modals: *May* and *Might*   149

Unit 12 Comparisons   166

Unit 13 Past Progressive; Direct and Indirect Objects   185

Unit 14 Modals: *Should, Had better, Have to; Must;* Superlatives   202

Putting It All Together   218

Answer Key   AK 1

About the Author

Samuela Eckstut has taught ESL and EFL for eighteen years, in the United States and in Greece, Italy, and England. Currently she is teaching at Boston University, Center for English Language and Orientation Programs (CELOP). She has authored or co-authored numerous texts for the teaching of English, notably *What's in a Word? Reading and Vocabulary Building, In the Real World, Interlink, First Impressions, Beneath the Surface,* and *Widely Read.*

A SIMPLE PAST TENSE: REGULAR VERBS: AFFIRMATIVE AND NEGATIVE STATEMENTS

Simple Past Tense

A.1

Match the situation with the best sentence.

1. __d__ Sylvia is tired.

2. __i__ Sylvia's worried about her French test.

3. __a__ Sylvia's car is clean.

4. __e__ Sylvia is hungry.

5. __g__ Sylvia's teacher is angry with her.

6. __b__ Sylvia is happy.

7. __c__ Sylvia's talking to a friend about a TV program.

8. __d__ Sylvia feels bad.

9. __h__ There's a lot of food in Sylvia's refrigerator.

a. She washed it yesterday.

b. Her boyfriend called her ten times yesterday to say, "I love you."

c. She watched it last night.

d. She didn't sleep much last night.

e. She didn't eat breakfast or lunch.

f. She didn't visit her grandparents.

g. She arrived late to class today.

h. She cooked a lot yesterday.

i. She didn't study very much.

A.2

Complete the sentences. Use **yesterday** *or* **last**.

Detective's Notes on Mr. Horace Smith	
April 15th	Traveled to Vancouver
April 25th	Borrowed $20,000
May 13th	Moved into a new apartment
	(Nothing unusual until May 19th)
May 19th	
7:00 A.M.	Arrived at work
2:00 P.M.	Finished work
6:00 P.M.	Returned to the office
11:00 P.M.	Visited someone at a hotel

It's Thursday, May 20th. Here's our report on Horace Smith.

_____Last_____ month he traveled to Vancouver. _____last_____ month he also
   1.   2.
borrowed $20,000 from the bank. _____Last_____ week he moved into a new apartment.
                                         3.
_____Yesterday_____ morning he arrived at work at seven o'clock. At two o'clock _____
     4.   5.
afternoon he finished work. Then something strange happened. He returned to the office at six o'clock
_____Last_____ evening and visited someone at a hotel at eleven o'clock _____last_____
     6.   7.
night.

A.3

Answer the questions.

a. What day of the week is it today? _Today is Sunday_ 8

b. What month is it now? _October_

c. What year is it now? _2,000_

*Use the answers above to rewrite the sentences. Use **ago**.*

> *Example: Eric cleaned his apartment last Sunday. (It is Tuesday.)*
>
> *Eric cleaned his apartment two days ago.*

1. Eric traveled to Poland in 1991.

   Eric traveled to Poland eigth years ago.

2. Eric visited his college roommate last July.

   Eric visited his college roommate two months ago.

3. Eric called his parents last Monday.

   Eric called his parents one month ago

4. Eric talked to his boss about a raise last Friday.

   _____

5. Eric graduated from college in 1988.

   Eric graduated from college 12 years ago

6. Eric moved to Georgia last December.

   Eric moved to Georgia 10 months ago

7. Eric played tennis last Thursday.

   Eric played tennis three days ago

8. Eric studied Polish in 1989.

   Eric studied polish eleven years ago

9. Eric's grandfather died last September.

   Eric's grandfather died one months ago

A.4

Complete the sentences.

1. Pete walks to work every day.

   He walked to work _____ yesterday, too.

2. Lenny, Mike, and Warren play basketball every Saturday.

   They played basketball _____ last Saturday, too.

(Continued on next page.)

3. Ellen washes her clothes every Sunday.

   She washed her clothes last Sunday, too.

4. My classmates study every night.

   My classmates studied last night, too.

5. Robert works in his garden every weekend.

   He worked in his garden last weekend, too.

6. Norma prepares dinner at 6:00 every day.

   She prepared dinner yesterday, too.

7. Anna talks to her daughter every Friday night.

   She talked to her daughter last Friday night, too.

8. Michele and her husband travel to France every summer.

   They traveled to France last summer, too.

9. The bank closes at 3:00 P.M. every day.

   It closed at 3:00 pm. yesterday, too.

10. Adam and his sister watch television every night.

    They watched t.v. last night, too.

A.5

Complete the sentences. Use the correct form of the verbs in parentheses.

1. I (wash) _washed_ the clothes this morning, but I (not wash) _didn't wash_ the

   dishes.

2. We (invite) _invited_ the Hangs to our party last week, but we (not invite)

   didn't invite the Lees.

3. I (clean) _cleaned_ the kitchen yesterday, but I (not clean) _didn't clean_ the

   bathroom.

4. Last night I (talk) _talked_ to my aunt, but I (not talk) _didn't talk_ to my

   uncle.

5. I (call) _called_ your brother a few minutes ago, but I (not call) _didn't call_

   you.

6. We (watch) ___watched___ television last night, but we (not watch) ___didn't___ the news.

7. Mr. Lugo (return) ___returned___ his book to the library today, but Mrs. Lugo (not return) ___didn't returns___ hers.

8. The artist (paint) ___painted___ a picture of her sister, but she (not paint) ___didn't paint___ a picture of her brother.

9. I (cook) ___cooked___ some potatoes, but I (not cook) ___didn't cook___ any meat.

10. I (study) ___studied___ history in high school, but I (not study) ___didn't study___ geography.

A.6

Complete the letter. Use the simple present tense, present progressive, or simple past tense of the verbs in parentheses.

April 12th

Dear Amira,

I (sit) __sit__ at my desk, and I (think) __am thinking__ of you. I often
      1.   2.
(think) __think__ of you on days like today. The sun (shine) __shines__, and
          3.   4.
the birds (sing) __sing__.
                  5.

The weather's very different from the weather yesterday. It (rain) __rained__ all day
                                                                        6.
long and I (stay) __stayed__ in the house from morning until night. I (not go)
                  7.
__didn't go__ out at all. I (wash) __washed__ the clothes and (clean)
      8.   9.
__cleaned__ the house—very exciting! After dinner I (play) __played__ cards with
    10.   11.
some neighbors.

One of my neighbors, Alfredo, (come) __came__ from Argentina. Sometimes I (speak)
                                        12.
__speak__ Spanish with him. I (not speak) __don't speak__ Spanish very well, but
    13.   14.
Alfredo is very nice and never (laugh) __laugh__ at my mistakes.
                                        15.

Last week he (invite) __invited__ me to an Argentinian party. We (listen)
                      16.
__listened__ to beautiful music all night and I (dance) __danced__ a lot. I really
    17.   18.
(enjoy) __enjoyed__ myself.
          19.

Well, it's time to go. I (cook) __cook__ some Argentinian food, and I (need)
                                20.
__need__ to check it. I (not want) __didn't want__ it to burn. You and I both (know)
    21.   22.
__know__ that I'm not a very good cook!
    23.

Write soon!

Love,

Connie

B SIMPLE PAST TENSE: IRREGULAR VERBS: AFFIRMATIVE AND NEGATIVE STATEMENTS

B.1

Underline the verb in each sentence. Write **regular** *if the simple past tense form is regular. Write* **irregular** *if the simple past tense form is irregular. Then write the base form of the verb.*

1. This morning I <u>got</u> up at seven o'clock.   *irregular*   *get*

2. I <u>washed</u> my face and hands.   *regular*   *wash*

3. Then I put on my clothes.   *irregular*   *put*

4. I had orange juice and toast for breakfast.   *regular*   *have*

5. After breakfast I brushed my teeth.   *regular*   *brush*

6. I left the house at 7:45.   *"*   *leave*

7. I arrived at school at 8:15.   *"*   *arrive*

8. Class began at 8:30.   *"*   *begin*

9. We learned some new grammar rules in class today.   *"*   *learn*

10. Class finished at 11:30.   *finish*

11. I met some friends for lunch.   *meet*

12. We ate at a pizza place.   *eat*

13. After lunch we went to a swimming pool.   *go*

14. We stayed there until four o'clock.   *stay*

B.2

Complete each sentence with the correct form of the verb.

1. I didn't eat eggs for breakfast. I _____*ate*_____ cereal.

2. We didn't drink coffee. We _____*drank*_____ tea.

3. He didn't leave at six o'clock. He _____*left*_____ at seven.

4. She didn't meet her sister at the movies. She _____*met*_____ her brother.

5. I didn't speak to the waiter. I _____*spoke*_____ to the manager.

(Continued on next page.)

6. I didn't go to the supermarket on Walnut Street. I _____went_____ to the supermarket on

   Chestnut Street.

7. The thief didn't steal my money. He _____stole_____ my jewelry.
ladron

8. I didn't find your keys. I _____found_____ your address book.

9. We didn't drive to the park. We _____drove_____ to the beach.

10. I didn't see Carol. I _____saw_____ Yoko.

11. My husband didn't bring me flowers. He _____brought_____ me chocolates.

12. We didn't come by bus. We _____came_____ by taxi.

B.3

Write true sentences.

1. I/become/an English teacher/last year

   I didn't become an English teacher last year.

2. I/eat/three kilos of oranges for breakfast/yesterday morning

   I didn't eat three kilos of oranges for breakfast yesterday m.

3. I/sleep/twenty-one hours/yesterday

   I didn't sleep twenty-one hours yesterday

4. I/bring/a horse to English class/two weeks ago

   I didn't bring a horse to English class two weeks ago.

5. I/go/to the moon/last month

   I didn't go to the moon last night

6. I/meet/the leader of my country/last night

   I didn't meet the leader of my country last night

7. I/find/$10,000 in a brown paper bag/yesterday

   I didn't find $10,000.00 in a brown paper bag yesterday

8. I/do/this exercise/two years ago

   I didn't do this exercise two years aago

9. I/swim/thirty kilometers/yesterday

I didn't swim thirty kilometers yesterday

10. I/speak/English perfectly/ten years ago

I didn't speak English perfectly ten years ago.

B.4

Complete the diary. Use the simple past tense form of the verbs in parentheses.

I (have) _had_ a nice day today. I (not get) _didn't get_ up until ten
o'clock, so I (get) _got_ dressed quickly and (go) _went_ to the Fine
Arts Museum.

I (meet) _met_ Cindy and Frank there, and we (go) _went_ into the
museum to see a new exhibit. We (not see) _didn't see_ everything because we (not have)
didn't have enough time. The exhibit (close) _closed_ at one o'clock. We (eat)
ate at a Chinese restaurant near the museum, and then we (take)
were taking a bus to the Downtown Shopping Mall. We (stay) _were staying_ at the
mall for a couple of hours and (look) _looked_ around. I (buy) _bought_ a
new shirt, but Frank and Cindy (not buy) _didn't buy_ anything.

Cindy and Frank (come) _didn't come_ back home with me, and I (make)
made dinner here. I (not have) _didn't have_ much in the refrigerator, so I
(drive) _drove_ to the supermarket to get some things. I (see) _saw_
Ramon there and (invite) _invited_ him for dinner, too.

We (not eat) _didn't eat_ until late, and after dinner we (watch) _were watching_ a
video. Ramon, Cindy, and Frank (not leave) _didn't leave_ until after midnight.

It's one o'clock in the morning now, and I'm tired. It's time to go to bed. Good night!

C SIMPLE PAST TENSE:
YES/NO QUESTIONS AND SHORT ANSWERS

C.1

Answer the questions. Use short answers. (Look at the conversation on page 206 of your grammar book if you need help.)

1. Did Carol have Thanksgiving dinner with her family?

   No, she didn't.

2. Did Carol and Yoko go to San Francisco for Thanksgiving?

   _____

3. Did Elenore make a turkey for Thanksgiving?

   _____

4. Did Pete prepare anything for the Thanksgiving dinner?

   _____

5. Did Norma have Thanksgiving dinner with her family?

   _____

6. Did Pete and Uncle Bob have a fight on Thanksgiving?

   _____

7. Did Uncle Bob like Pete's soup?

   _____

8. Did Pete and Elenore have Thanksgiving dinner at their home?

   _____

9. Did Uncle Bob watch a football game on television?

   _____

C.2

There's a mistake in each question. Write the question without the mistake.

1. You did finish the last exercise?

Did you finish the last exercise?

2. Did you all the homework?

Did you do all the homework?

3. You did took a bath this morning?

Did you take a bath this morning?

4. Does your best friend come over to your house last night?

Did your best friend come over to your house last night?

5. Did you went to bed early last night?

Did you go to bed early last night?

6. Did your English teacher taught you new grammar last week?

Did your English teacher teach you new grammar last week?

7. Do you visit the United States ten years ago?

Did you visit the United States ten years ago?

8. Your mother and father got married a long time ago?

Did your mother and father get married a long time

9. Did you watched television last night?

Did you watch tv. last night?

C.3

Answer the questions in exercise C.2. Use short answers.

1. (Did you finish the last exercise?)

Yes, I did.

2. Yes, I did.

3. Yes, I did.

4. No, he didn't.

5. No, I don't

6. Yes, she did.

7. Yes, I did.

8. No, they didn't.

9. No, I don't

C.4

Look at Sharon's list. Write her husband's questions. Then complete each answer with the simple past tense form of the verbs in parentheses.

Things To Do
Get the clothes from the dry cleaner's
Buy food for dinner
Meet Glen for lunch
Write a letter to Rena
Go to the bank
Return the book to the library
Look for a birthday present for Jane
Call the doctor
Bake some cookies
Pick the children up at 4:00

Sharon: Steven, you always say I forget to do things. Well, today I remembered to do everything.

Steven: Are you sure? Let's see your list. *Did you get the clothes from the dry cleaner's?*
1.

Sharon: Uh-huh. I (put) _____*put*_____ them in the closet.
2.

Steven: *Did you buy food for dinner?*
3.

Sharon: Yes, I did. I (get) _____*got*_____ some chicken, some vegetables, and some apples for
4.

dessert.

Steven: *Did you meet Glen for lunch?*
5.

Sharon: Yeah. We (eat) _____*ate*_____ at a great Thai restaurant.
6.

Steven: *Did you write a letter to Rena?*
7.

Sharon: Yes. I (mail) _____*mailed*_____ it at the post office.
8.

Steven: *Did you go to the bank?*
9.

Sharon: Yes, I did. I (deposit) _____*deposited*_____ both of the checks.
10.

Steven: *Did you return the book to the library?*
11.

Sharon: Yes, I did. And I (take) _____*took*_____ out another book by the same author.
12.

Steven: _Did you look for a birthday present for Jane_
                                                    13.
Sharon: Yeah. I (buy) _bought_ her a sweater.
                                    14.
Steven: _Did you call the doctor?_
                                    15.
Sharon: Uh-huh. He (say) _said_ all the test results are fine.
                                    16.
Steven: _Did you bake some cookies?_
                                                    17.
Sharon: Of course. And I (have) _have_ a few already. They're delicious.
                                                    18.
Steven: _Did you pick the children up at 4:00?_
                                                    19.
Sharon: Oh no, I (forget) _forgot_! What time is it?
                                    20.

D SIMPLE PAST TENSE: WH- QUESTIONS

D.1

Match the questions and answers about Carol and Yoko's Thanksgiving holiday. (Be careful! There is one extra answer.)

1. __h__ Who drove from Oregon to San Francisco?

2. __k__ Where did Yoko and Carol rent the car?

3. __d__ When did Yoko and Carol arrive in San Francisco?

4. __a__ How long did it take to drive from Oregon to San Francisco?

5. __i__ What did they do on Thursday?

6. __b__ Where did they walk on Friday?

7. __j__ Who did they walk around Berkeley with?

8. __g__ Who invited Yoko and Carol to his home?

9. __c__ When did Carol write her grandmother?

10. __f__ Why didn't Carol and Yoko visit Yoko's uncle?

a. More than six hours.

b. Around Berkeley.

c. On Sunday.

d. On Wednesday night.

e. Because they didn't bring their books.

f. Because they didn't want to drive anymore.

g. Yoko's uncle.

h. Yoko and Carol did.

i. They visited Fisherman's Wharf and Chinatown.

j. Yoko's friends.

k. In Oregon.

D.2

Write questions. Then answer the questions. (If you need help, the answers are at the end of the exercise.)

1. Where/Americans/celebrate Thanksgiving/for the first time

   Where did Americans celebrate Thanksgiving for the first time?

   In Massachusetts.

2. When/a human being/walk on the moon/for the first time

   When did a human being walk on the moon for the first time?
   In 1969

3. What/William Shakespeare/write

   What did William Shakespeare write?
   plays like Romeo and Juliet

4. Where/the Olympic games/start

   Where did the Olympic games start?
   In Greece

5. Why/many people/go to California/in 1849

   Why did many people go to California in 1849
   they wanted to find gold.

6. How long/John Kennedy/live in the White House

   How long did John Kennedy live in the White House?
   Almost three years.

7. What/Alfred Hitchcock/make

   What did Alfred Hitchcock make?
   Movies

8. Why/the Chinese/build the Great Wall

Why did the Chinese build the Great Wall?
They wanted to keep foreigners out of the country.

9. How long/World War II/last in Europe

How long did world war II last in Europe
About six years.

10. When/Christopher Columbus/discover/America

When did Christopher Columbus discover America
in 1492

Almost three years.	Movies.
About six years.	Plays like *Romeo and Juliet*.
In 1969.	They wanted to keep foreigners out of the country.
In 1492.	They wanted to find gold.
In Greece.	
In Massachusetts.	

D.3

*Write questions. Use **who** and the verb in parentheses.*

1. **A:** Carol went to San Francisco.

   B: (go) _____*Who did she go*_____ with?

   A: With her roommate, Yoko.

   B: How did they go there?

   A: By car.

   B: (drive) _____*Who drove*_____?

   A: I don't know. Probably both of them.

2. **A:** Those are beautiful flowers. (give) ___*who gave*___ them to you?

   B: My boyfriend.

3. **A:** I went to a party at my old high school last night.

   B: (see) ___*who did you see*___ there?

(Continued on next page.)

4. **A:** You got a phone call a couple of minutes ago.

   B: (call) _who called_ ?

   A: A woman. Her name was Betty Kowalski.

5. **A:** Did you ever read the book *The Old Man and the Sea?*

   B: (write) _who wrote_ it?

   A: Ernest Hemingway.

6. **A:** Where are the children?

   B: At Ryan Santiago's house.

   A: (take) _who took_ them there?

   B: Ryan's mother.

7. **A:** My wife sent the money to your office a month ago.

   B: (send) _who did she send_ it to?

   A: Nicole Sanda.

8. **A:** The car is so clean. (clean) _who cleaned_ it?

   B: I took it to a car wash.

   A: It looks great.

9. **A:** Did you hear the news? Kay got married.

   B: Really? (marry) _who did she marry_ ?

   A: A guy from Oklahoma. I don't know his name.

10. **A:** My grandparents went to Arizona for two months last winter.

    B: (stay) _who did they stay_ with?

    A: My cousin, Howard. He has a big house there.

D.4

Complete the conversation. Write questions. Use **what, where, when, who,**
or **why.**

Police: There was a robbery last night, and someone said you did it.

Donald: That person's lying.

Police: Well, then. Tell us about your activities last night.

What did you do?

1.

Donald: We went to the movies.

Police: We? <u>Who did you go with</u>?
2.

Donald: A friend. Her name's Wendy Kaufman.

Police: <u>what time did you leave your home?</u>
<u>when did</u> 3. <u>you leave your home?</u>

Donald: I left home at around 5:30.

Police: <u>what time did the movie start?</u>
<u>when did the movie start ?</u>
4.

Donald: The movie started at 8:30.

Police: <u>why did you leave your house so early ?</u>
5.

Donald: I left my house so early because we had dinner before the movie.

Police: <u>where did you eat?</u>
6.

Donald: At Maxi's Steak House.

Police: <u>where did you meet your friend?</u>
7.

Donald: I met her at the restaurant.

Police: <u>what did you eat?</u>
8.

Donald: A steak. That's what everybody eats at Maxi's.

Police: We're not interested in everybody. We're only interested in you.
<u>who saw you ?</u>
9.

Donald: The waitress saw us, of course. And I talked to the manager, too.

Police: <u>why did you talk to the manager?</u>
10.

Donald: Because the steak was no good.

Police: <u>where did you go after dinner?</u>
11.

Donald: After dinner? To the movies. I told you that already.

Police: <u>what did you see?</u>
12.

Donald: *Wine and Roses.* You know, the movie with Kristie McNeil.

Police: <u>where did you see the movie?</u>
13.

Donald: At the Cinemax on Ocean Road.

A PAST TENSE OF *BE*: AFFIRMATIVE AND NEGATIVE STATEMENTS, *YES/NO* QUESTIONS, AND SHORT ANSWERS

A.1

Kim went shopping at Miller's Department Store. Complete the sentences about her purchases. Use **was** *or* **were**.

1. *The pants were $45.*

2. *The jacket was $79.99.*

3. the Shirt was 29.99

4. the tie was 16.00

5. the socks were 8.00

6. The Sweater was 39.00

7. the coat was 145.00

8. the pajamas were 19.99

9. The shorts were 14.99

10. the gloves were 25.00

11. the hat was 22.00

12. the shoes were 65.00

Pants	$45.00
Jacket	$79.99
Shirt	$29.99
Tie	$16.00
Socks	$8.00
Sweater	$39.00
Coat	$145.00
Pajamas	$19.99
Shorts	$14.99
Gloves	$25.00
Hat	$22.00
Shoes	$65.00

A.2

Write sentences. Use **was, wasn't, were,** *or* **weren't**.

1. Abraham Lincoln/born/in England

   Abraham Lincoln wasn't born in England.

2. Picasso and Michelangelo/painters

   Picasso and Michelangelo were painters.

3. William Shakespeare and Charles Dickens/Canadian

William Shakespeare and Charles Dickens weren't Canadian.

4. Ronald Reagan/the first president of the United States

Ronald Reagan wasn't the first president of the United States.

5. Charlie Chaplin and Marilyn Monroe/movie stars

Charlie Chaplin and Marilyn Monroe were movie stars.

6. The end of World War I/in 1922

The end of World War I wasn't in 1922.

7. *E.T.*/ the name of a movie

E.T. was the name of a movie.

8. Toronto and Washington, D.C./big cities 300 years ago

Toronto and Washington D.C. weren't big cities 300 years ago.

9. Indira Gandhi and Napoleon/famous people

Indira Gandhi and Napoleon were famous people.

10. Margaret Thatcher/a political leader

Margaret Thatcher was a political leader.

11. Oregon and Hawaii/part of the United States/in 1776

Oregon and Hawaii weren't part of the United States in 1776.

12. Disneyland/a famous place/100 years ago

Disneyland wasn't a famous place 100 years ago.

A.3

Answer the questions. Use short answers.

1. Was Carol with her family on Thanksgiving?

No, she wasn't.

2. Were your parents born in New York?

No, they weren't.

3. Were you a happy child?

Yes, I was.

4. Was your father a good student?

Yes, he was.

5. Was it cold yesterday?

No, it wasn't.

6. Were you born in a hospital?

Yes, I was.

Now answer these questions.

7. Was Yoko with Carol on Thanksgiving? — *Yes, she was.*

8. Did Carol and Yoko go to New York for Thanksgiving? — *No, they didn't.*

9. Were you and a friend at the movies last night? — Yes, we were.

10. Did you buy anything yesterday? — No, I didn't

11. Was the last grammar exercise easy? — No, it wasn't

12. Did you take a shower yesterday? — Yes, I did.

13. Did your English teacher give you a test last week? — No, she didn't

14. Were you absent from your last English class? — Yes, I was.

15. Did your parents get married five years ago? — No, they didn't

A.4

Write questions and answers. Use the past tense of **be**.

1. **A:** We had a nice holiday.

   B: (you/with your whole family) — *Were you with your whole family?*

   A: (no/my daughter/in Montreal) — *No, my daughter was in Montreal.*

2. **A:** I bought these new shoes yesterday.

   B: (they/on sale) — were they on sale?

   A: (yes/they/only $25) — Yes, they were only 25.00

3. **A:** (you/at home/last night) — were you at home last night?

   B: (no/I/at the library) — No, I was at the library.

4. **A:** (the guests/late for the party) — were the guests late for the party?

   B: (no/they/all on time) — No they were all on time

5. **A:** (it/warm/in Australia) — was it warm in Australia

   B: (the weather/beautiful/every day) — Yes, the weather was beautiful every day

6. **A:** (the movie/good) — Was the movie good?

   B: (it/okay) — Yes, it was okay.

7. **A:** (the people at the party/friendly) *were the people at the party friendly?*

   B: (most of them/very nice) *most of them, were very nice*

8. **A:** I called the lawyer.

   B: (he/there) *was he there?*

   A: (no/he/at a meeting) *No, he was at a meeting.*

A.5

Complete the conversation. Use **is, are, was,** *or* **were.**

A: It _____*is*_____ a beautiful day. The sun feels so good.
1.

B: Yes, it does—especially because the weather _____*was*_____ so terrible yesterday. The weather in
2.

this city _____*is*_____ so strange. One day it _____*is*_____ warm, and the next day it
3. 4.

_____*is*_____ cold.
5.

A: You _____*are*_____ right about that. In my country, it _____*is*_____ always warm and sunny.
6. 7.

B: _____*is*_____ warm in the winter, too?
8.

A: Uh-huh. It _____*is*_____ rarely colder than 70 degrees. This last Christmas I _____*was*_____ home
9. 10.

for two weeks, and it _____*was*_____ sunny and warm. My friends and I _____*were*_____ at the beach
11. 12.

every day. How about you? _____*were*_____ you here this past Christmas?
13.

B: Yeah. My parents _____*were*_____ here for a few days for a visit. We _____*were*_____ cold most of the
14. 15.

time, and my mother _____*was*_____ ill for a few days. They _____*were*_____ happy to see me, but
16. 17.

they _____*were*_____ glad to leave this awful weather.
18.

A: _____*are*_____ your parents back home now?
19.

B: No, they _____*are*_____ on another vacation—this time, in a warm place.
20.

B PAST TENSE OF *BE*: *WH-* QUESTIONS

B.1

Complete the conversations. Choose the correct question.

1. **A:** I was absent yesterday.

   B: *What was wrong?*

   a. Who was absent?
   b. What was wrong?

   A: I was ill.

2. **A:** We had dinner at the new Mexican restaurant.

   B: How was the food?

   a. How was the food?
   b. Where was the restaurant?

   A: Very good.

3. **A:** You forgot Cathy's birthday.

   B: when was it?

   a. When was it?
   b. Where was she?

   A: Last Thursday.

4. **A:** I went to bed at eight o'clock last night.

   B: why were you so tired?

   a. What did you do?
   b. Why were you so tired?

   A: I don't know. I didn't feel very well.

5. **A:** You missed a great party.

   B: who was there?

   a. Who was there?
   b. How was the party?

   A: People from our class and their friends.

6. **A:** I found your keys.

B: _____ *where were they?* _____

    a. Where were they?

    b. Why were they there?

A: Under the desk.

7. **A:** I got everything right on the test.

B: _____ *Really? What were the answers to the first and third question?* _____

    a. Really? Where were the answers to the first and third questions?

    b. Really? What were the answers to the first and third questions?

A: The answer to the first was C, and D was the answer to the third.

8. **A:** We were on vacation for two weeks.

B: _____ *How was it?* _____

    a. Why were you on vacation?

    b. How was it?

A: It was great.

9. **A:** We had a great time in Hong Kong.

B: _____ *when were you there?* _____

    a. Who were you with?

    b. When were you there?

A: We were there about two years ago.

B.2

Complete the questions. Use **was,** **were,** *or* **did.**

1. Why _____ *did* _____ you go there?

2. Who _____ *were* _____ you with?

3. What _____ *did* _____ you wear?

4. How _____ *was* _____ the weather?

5. Where _____ *were* _____ you yesterday?

6. How _____ *did* _____ you get to the beach?

7. Where _____ *was* _____ your husband?

8. When _____ *did* _____ he come home?

9. What ___was___ the problem with the bus?

10. Why ___was___ he angry?

11. Where ___did___ your friends meet you?

12. Why ___were___ your friends late?

B.3

Here are the answers to the questions in exercise B.2. Match the questions and answers.

1. *Where were you yesterday?*   At the beach.

2. _How was the weather?_   It was beautiful.

3. _How did you get to the beach?_ By bus.

4. _What was the problem with the bus?_ It was crowded.

5. _Why did you go there?_   We wanted to swim.

6. _Who were you with?_   Some friends.

7. _Where did your friends meet you?_ At the bus station.

8. _Why were your friends late?_ They woke up late.

9. _What did you wear?_   My new bathing suit.

10. _Where was your husband_   At his office.

11. _Why was he angry?_   He didn't go to the beach with us.

12. _When did he come home?_ Late last night.

B.4

*Complete the conversations. Write the correct questions. Use **was** or **were**.*

1. **A:** Did you pay a lot of money for those sunglasses?

   B: No, they were on sale.

   A: When _were they on sale_ ?

   B: Last week.

2. **A:** I tried to call you last night.

   B: I wasn't home.

   A: Where _was you last night_ ?

   B: At a friend's apartment.

3. **A:** Did you have your history test yesterday?

   B: No, we had it today.

   A: How _was it_ ?

   B: It was okay, but I didn't know the answers to two of the questions.

4. **A:** Did the kids go swimming?

   B: No, they were afraid.

   A: Why _were they afraid_ ?

   B: The water was deep.

5. **A:** Did you go to the basketball game?

   B: Yeah, it was a great game.

   A: What _was the score_ ?.

   B: I don't remember the score, but our team won.

6. **A:** Those are beautiful shoes. Where did you get them?

   B: At a store on Washington Street.

   A: What _was the name of the store_

   B: I think the name of the store was Dalton's. Or, was it Dillon's?

7. **A:** Did your dog have her puppies yet?

   B: She sure did—six of them.

   A: When _were they born_ ?

   B: They were born a few days ago.

8. **A:** What's new?

   B: The police were here.

   A: Why _were they here_ ?

   B: Someone called them, but I don't know why.

9. **A:** You were brave to go there alone.

   B: I wasn't alone.

   A: Who _was with you_ ?

   B: My brother and sister.

10. **A:** Did you ever read this book?

    B: Yes, it was about Eleanor Roosevelt.

    A: Who _was she_ ?

    B: She was the wife of President Roosevelt.

11. **A:** Do you know this school, the Foreign Language Institute?

    B: Yes, I took a couple of German classes there last year.

    A: How _was_ ?

    B: Both of my teachers were very good.

C PAST OF *BE*: *THERE WAS/THERE WERE*

C.1

Put a check (✓) next to the statements that are true.

In the eighteenth century:

1. There weren't any televisions. _✓_

2. There weren't any horses. _____

3. There were houses. _✓_

4. There wasn't any water. _____

5. There were radios. _____

6. There was a war. _____

7. There weren't any car accidents. _____

8. There weren't any pianos. _____

9. There was cold weather. _____

10. There were telephones. _____

C.2

Do you remember Unit 2 of your grammar book? Complete the description.
Use **there was** *or* **there were**.

1. *there was* _____ a picture of a man at an eye doctor's office.

2. *there were* _____ some grammar exercises.

3. _____ a conversation between Lulu and a woman at a laundromat.

4. _____ a letter from Carol to her grandmother.

5. _____ grammar notes.

6. _____ two pictures of desks.

7. _____ a story.

8. _____ many questions.

9. _____ lots of things to do.

10. _____ a description of Carol's family.

C.3

Complete the sentences about the newspaper headlines. Use **there was, there wasn't, there were,** *or* **there weren't.**

PLANE CRASH KILLS TWO

Bank Robbery At Freedom Savings

Two robbers get away with $50,000

Lorem ipsum dolor sit amet, consectetuer adipiscing elit, sed diam nonummy nibh euismod tincidunt ut laoreet dolore magna aliquam erat

volutpat. Ut wis quis nostrud ex suscipit loborti ullamcorper su nibh euismod ti magna aliquam enim ad minim exerci tation ulla

No Classes At Norton Community College
Fight between students

• FIRE AT CENTRAL ELEMENTARY SCHOOL •
NO INJURIES REPORTED

Car Accident Injures Five

— NO —
BASEBALL GAMES YESTERDAY
Players' one-day strike is over

MEETING BETWEEN LEADERS OF THE U.S. AND CHINA
Discussions about many important problems

Earthquake In British Columbia
No reports of deaths or injuries

1. *There was* _____ a plane crash. *There were* _____ two deaths.

2. _____ a fire at Central Elementary School. _____ any injuries.

3. _____ a bank robbery at Freedom Savings Bank. _____ two robbers.

4. _____ a car accident. _____ five injuries.

5. _____ any classes at Norton Community College because _____ a

   fight between students.

6. _____ a meeting between the leaders of the United States and China.

   _____ discussions about many important problems.

7. _____ an earthquake in British Columbia, but _____ any reports of

   deaths or injuries.

8. _____ any baseball games yesterday. _____ a strike.

C.4

Answer the questions. Use short answers.

1. Was there a fire near your home yesterday? _____

2. Were there enough chairs for everyone in your last

   English class? _____

3. Was there a good program on TV last night? _____

4. Was there a break during your last English class? _____

5. Were there any visitors at your home late last night? _____

6. Were there any problems in your town last week? _____

7. Was there a test in your English class last week? _____

8. Were there any letters in the mail for you last week? _____

C.5

Complete the conversation. Write questions. Use the words in the box.

cheap restaurants?	a casino on the island?
a view of the sea from your hotel room?	many places to go shopping?
a lot of tourists?	many English-speaking people?
interesting things to see?	a beach near the hotel?
a restaurant in the hotel?	

A: I hear you went to the Caribbean for your vacation.

B: Yes, we did. It was wonderful.

A: *Were there a lot of tourists?* _____
                                                    1.

B: No, we were surprised. There weren't many people at all.

A: How was your hotel?

B: It wasn't bad. It was on the sea and it wasn't too expensive.

A: _____
                                    2.

B: Yes, it was beautiful. It was nice to wake up in the morning and see hundreds of boats outside our

   window.

A: _____
                                    3.

B: Yes, we had breakfast there every morning.

A: _____
4.

B: Yes, but it wasn't very clean. We never went swimming there.

A: _____
5.

B: Uh-huh. We never spent too much money on lunch or dinner.

A: _____
6.

B: Yes. We went somewhere different every day.

A: _____
7.

B: There were a few tourist shops near the big hotels. They had postcards, T-shirts—things like that.

A: _____
8.

B: No, there weren't. Most of the people spoke only French.

A: _____
9.

B: I don't know. We don't like to gamble, and we always went to bed early.

A COUNT AND NON-COUNT NOUNS AND QUANTIFIERS

A.1

Look at the store signs. Write the correct aisle number.

 1 Eggs   Butter
Juice   Cheese
Milk

 4 Toilet Paper
Paper Towels
Napkins
Plastic Bags

 7 Frozen Food
Ice Cream

 2 Bread
Rolls

 5 Potato Chips
Cookies
Cereal

8 Canned Vegetables
Canned Fish
Rice

 3 Toothbrushes
Toothpaste
Soap
Shampoo

 6 Sugar
Flour
Salt

9 Fresh Fruit

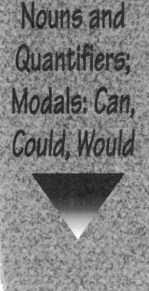

1. <u>Sugar</u> is in aisle __6__.

2. <u>Cookies</u> are in aisle _____.

3. <u>Ice cream</u> is in aisle _____.

4. <u>Eggs</u> are in aisle _____.

5. <u>Fruit</u> is in aisle _____.

6. Canned <u>vegetables</u> are in aisle _____.

7. <u>Napkins</u> are in aisle _____.

8. <u>Milk</u> is in aisle _____.

9. <u>Rice</u> is in aisle _____.

10. Plastic <u>bags</u> are in aisle _____.

11. <u>Potato chips</u> are in aisle _____.

12. Frozen <u>food</u> is in aisle _____.

13. <u>Bread</u> is in aisle _____.

14. Canned <u>fish</u> is in aisle _____.

15. <u>Toothbrushes</u> are in aisle _____.

U N I T

10

Nouns and Quantifiers; Modals: Can, Could, Would

A.2

Write the underlined words in exercise A.1 in the correct column.

COUNT NOUNS	NON-COUNT NOUNS
cookies	sugar

A.3

Find the twelve mistakes in the list of count nouns and non-count nouns.
*Circle them. Then write the list again. Write **a**, **an**, or **some** before each word.*

COUNT NOUNS	NON-COUNT NOUNS	COUNT NOUNS	NON-COUNT NOUNS
egg	books	an egg	some bread
(bread)	food	some books	some food
furniture	water		
student	people		
money	paper		
information	uncle		
teeth	homework		
rain	advice		
children	television		
friends	traffic		
oil	questions		
animal	computer		

A.4

Complete the sentences. Choose the correct words.

1. Do you have _____ *a pencil* _____?
   a. some pencil
   b. a pencil

2. The _____ on the table.
   a. money is
   b. money are

3. There _____ in the refrigerator.
   a. is some fruit
   b. are some fruits

4. We don't have _____.
   a. much book
   b. many books

5. Do you want _____?
   a. an apple
   b. some apple

6. I'm sorry I'm late. The _____ terrible.
   a. traffic was
   b. traffics were

7. Do you like Chinese _____?
   a. food
   b. foods

8. Do you have _____?
   a. a water
   b. any water

9. Is there _____ in the bedroom?
   a. a radio
   b. any radio

10. Don't rush! We have a lot of _____.
    a. time
    b. times

11. I want _____.
    a. an information
    b. some information

A.5

Jack did some Sunday morning shopping. He brought some things on his shopping list, but he didn't buy everything. Write sentences about what he bought and about what he did not buy. Use **some, any,** *or* **a.**

Shopping List

~~Bananas~~   Toothbrush

Cheese   ~~Potatoes~~

~~Orange juice~~   Lettuce

Lemons   Carrots

~~Newspaper~~   ~~Butter~~

Bread   ~~Milk~~

Onions   ~~Eggs~~

1. *He bought some bananas.*
2. *He didn't buy any cheese.*
3. _____
4. _____
5. _____
6. _____
7. _____
8. _____
9. _____
10. _____
11. _____
12. _____
13. _____
14. _____

A.6

Write ten true sentences. Use words from each column.

I have	a lot of a little a few	cheese in my pocket food in my refrigerator money in my pocket books next to my bed shirts in my closet friends
I don't have	much many any	free time children work to do today questions for my teacher jewelry medicine in my bathroom problems with English grammar photographs in my wallet ice cream at home

Example: *I don't have any cheese in my pocket.*

1. _____

2. _____

3. _____

4. _____

5. _____

6. _____

7. _____

8. _____

9. _____

10. _____

B COUNT AND NON-COUNT NOUNS: *YES/NO* QUESTIONS; QUESTIONS ABOUT QUANTITY: *HOW MUCH* AND *HOW MANY*

B.1

Match the containers and non-count nouns.

1. a can of	a. lettuce
2. a carton of	b. soda
3. a head of	c. bread
4. a loaf of	d. milk

Do the same with these words.

5. a bottle of	e. cake
6. a box of	f. cigarettes
7. a pack of	g. juice
8. a piece of	h. cereal

Do the same with these words, too.

9. a bar of	i. toothpaste
10. a jar of	j. toilet paper
11. a roll of	k. jam
12. a tube of	l. soap

B.2

Look at Tina's cash register receipt and answer the questions.

1. How much soda did she buy?

   Six cans

2. How many loaves of bread did she buy?

   One

3. How much milk did she buy?

   _____

6 Soda	$2.19
1 Bread	$1.05
1 Milk	$1.19
2 Lettuce	$3.58
3 Apple juice	$5.40
1 Cereal	$2.29
4 Toilet paper	$1.69
3 Soap	$2.45
1 Toothpaste	$2.39
2 Jam	$3.38
TOTAL	**$25.61**

THANK YOU FOR SHOPPING
AT CASTLE'S

4. How much lettuce did she buy?

_____

5. How many bottles of apple juice did she buy?

_____

6. How many boxes of cereal did she buy?

_____

7. How much toilet paper did she buy?

_____

8. How much soap did she buy?

_____

9. How much toothpaste did she buy?

_____

10. How many jars of jam did she buy?

_____

B.3

Write questions. Use **a, an,** *or* **any.**

1. telephone/in your bedroom

   Is there a telephone in your bedroom?

2. flowers/in a vase in your home

   Are there any flowers in a vase in your home?

3. trash/in your kitchen

   Is there any trash in your kitchen?

4. furniture/in your home

   _____

5. clothes/in your closet

   _____

6. money/under your bed

   _____

7. alarm clock/next to your bed

_____

8. snow/on the ground outside your home

_____

9. sink/in your bathroom

_____

10. dishes/in your kitchen sink

_____

11. pictures/on the walls of your bedroom

_____

12. candy/in your home

_____

13. window/in your kitchen

_____

14. television/in your living room

_____

B.4

Answer the questions in exercise B.3. Use short answers.

1. _____

2. _____

3. _____

4. _____

5. _____

6. _____

7. _____

8. _____

9. _____

10. _____

11. _____

12. _____

13. _____

14. _____

B.5

Write questions. Use **how many** *or* **how much**.

A: Are you going to the store?

B: Yes, why?

A: I need some things. I need some cheese.

B: *How much cheese do you need?*
1.

A: About a pound. And I want some eggs.

B: *How many eggs do you want?*
2.

A: A dozen. I also need some flour.

B: _____
3.

A: One pound, I think.

B: Do you want any sugar?

A: No, I have sugar.

B: _____
4.

A: A few cups, at least. But I want some bananas.

B: _____
5.

A: Five or six. I want some oranges, too.

B: _____
6.

A: A few. Oh, and I need some rice.

B: _____
7.

A: A box. I also need some potatoes.

B: _____
8.

A: Get about ten. Oh, one more thing. I want some milk.

B: _____
9.

(Continued on next page.)

A: Half a gallon. Oh, don't forget to get some flowers. I want roses.

B: _____
                                    10.

A: Half a dozen.

B: Is that it? Are you sure you don't want any cookies?

A: No, I have enough cookies.

B: _____
                                    11.

A: Two dozen. Here, let me give you some money.

B: I have money.

A: _____
                                    12.

B: About twenty dollars.

A: Here. Take another twenty.

C ENOUGH + NOUN; *TOO MUCH/TOO MANY/ TOO LITTLE/TOO FEW* + NOUN

C.1

Complete the sentences. Choose the correct words.

1. What did the student say to the teacher?

   "I didn't finish the homework. I ___*didn't have enough*___ time."
   a. had too much
   b. didn't have enough

2. What did the driver say to the passenger in her car?

   "We _____ gas. We need to go to the gas station."
   a. have too much
   b. don't have enough

3. What did the passenger in the car say to the driver?

   "There _____ cars. Let's go to another parking lot."
   a. are too many
   b. aren't enough

4. What did the cashier at the drugstore say to the little girl?

"I'm sorry. You have _____ money. Go home and get some more."
a. too much
b. too little

5. Ted and Niki wanted to see a movie, but there was a long line for tickets. What did Ted say?

"There are _____ people. Let's go and see another movie."
a. too many
b. too few

6. What did the doctor say to his patient?

"You said you're on a diet, but you lost only one pound last month. That

_____ weight."
a. is too much
b. isn't enough

7. What did the photography teacher say to the student?

"This picture is dark. You had _____ light."
a. too much
b. too little

8. What did Mitchell's mother say to him?

"You ate _____ fruit. That's why you have a stomachache."
a. too much
b. too little

9. What did the customer say to the waitress?

"There are _____ forks on the table for six people.
a. too many
b. too few

Please bring some more."

10. What did Debbie say to her roommate?

"You bought _____ juice. There's no place to put all
a. too much
b. too little

these bottles."

C.2

Write sentences about the pictures. Use **not enough, too much,** *or* **too many** *and the words in the box.*

air	birds	days	furniture	people	toothpaste
batteries	chairs	food	numbers	shampoo	water

1.

There are too many

people in the boat.

2.

FEBRUARY

S	M	T	W	T	F	S
1	2	3	4	5	6	7
8	9	10	11	12	13	14
15	16	17	18	19	20	21
22	23	24	25	26	27	28
29	30	31				

3.

4.

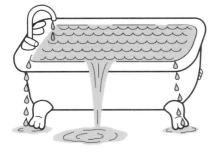

5.

6.

7.

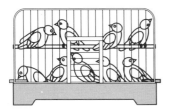

8.

9.

10.

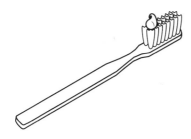

_____

_____

11.

_____

_____

12.

_____

_____

C.3

Rewrite the sentences. Use **too little** _or_ **too few.**

1. We don't have enough chairs.

   We have too few chairs.

2. There isn't enough salt in this soup.

   There's too little salt in this soup.

3. There weren't enough people for two teams.

   _____

4. We didn't have enough paper for everyone in the class.

   _____

5. There wasn't enough food for fifteen people.

   _____

6. You don't have enough information.

   _____

7. There aren't enough bedrooms in that apartment.

   _____

8. We didn't have enough time for the test.

   _____

(Continued on next page.)

9. These aren't enough bananas for a banana cake.

_____

10. There aren't enough salespeople at that store.

_____

D MODALS: *CAN* AND *COULD* FOR ABILITY AND POSSIBILITY; *MAY I, CAN I,* AND *COULD I* FOR POLITE REQUESTS

D.1

Look at the job advertisements and the qualifications of Martha, Frank, Les, and Rosa. Then answer the questions.

WANTED
SECRETARY
Type 70 words per minute.
Need to speak Spanish.

WANTED
•SUMMER BABYSITTER•
Take two small children to the beach every day.
Also, go horseback riding with ten-year-old girl.

DRIVER WANTED
Drive truck to airport every day.
Pick up boxes and deliver to downtown offices.

WANTED
SUMMER CAMP WORKER
◆ Teach children the guitar.
◆ Also work with children in art class

	MARTHA	FRANK	LES	ROSA
draw	no	no	yes	yes
drive	yes	no	yes	no
lift 100 pounds	no	no	yes	yes
play the guitar	no	yes	no	yes
ride a horse	yes	no	no	no
speak Spanish	no	yes	no	yes
swim	yes	yes	no	yes
type	yes	yes	no	no

1. Which job is good for Martha? The job as *summer babysitter* _____

2. Which job is good for Frank? The job as _____

3. Which job is good for Les? The job as _____

4. Which job is good for Rosa? The job as _____

D.2

Look at the information in exercise D.1 again. Then answer the questions.
Use **can** *or* **can't**.

1. Why is the job as babysitter good for Martha?

   She *can swim and ride a horse.* _____

2. Why isn't the job as babysitter good for Rosa?

   She *can swim, but she can't ride a horse.* _____

3. Why isn't the job as babysitter good for Les?

   He *can't swim, and he can't ride a horse.* _____

4. Why is the job as driver good for Les?

   He _____

5. Why is the job as secretary good for Frank?

   He _____

6. Why is the job as summer camp worker good for Rosa?

   She _____

7. Why isn't the job as driver good for Frank?

   _____

8. Why isn't the job as secretary good for Martha?

   _____

9. Why isn't the job as driver good for Rosa?

   _____

10. Why isn't the job as summer camp worker good for Les?

    _____

11. Why isn't the job as summer camp worker good for Martha?

    _____

12. Why isn't the job as secretary good for Les?

    _____

D.3

Write questions. Use **can**.

1. you/drive   *Can you drive?* _____

2. your mother/lift 100 pounds   _____

3. your father/play the guitar   _____

4. your best friend/ride a horse   _____

5. your parents/speak Spanish   _____

6. you/swim   _____

7. you/type   _____

D.4

Answer the questions in exercise D.3. Use short answers.

1. _____

2. _____

3. _____

4. _____

5. _____

6. _____

7. _____

D.5

Complete the sentences. Use **could** *or* **couldn't** *and the verbs in parentheses.*

1. I'm sorry that I (call) _____ *couldn't call* _____ you yesterday. I was very busy.

2. We enjoyed our holiday in Spain because we (practice) _____ our Spanish.

3. We (go) _____ to the party last night. Our son was ill.

4. I didn't answer the questions. I (understand) _____ the story.

5. I had a terrible stomachache yesterday. I (eat) _____ a thing.

6. In high school I had a lot of free time. I (play) _____ soccer with my friends

   every Saturday and Sunday.

7. We didn't meet our friends for dinner last night. We (find) _____ the restaurant.

8. Our room in that hotel was terrible. We (hear) _____ the people in the other room all the time.

9. We don't have photographs from the museum. It was dark and we (use) _____ a flash.

10. I liked my summer job. I (do) _____ what I wanted.

D.6

Make polite requests. Use **may I** *or* **can I**.

1. You have a doctor's appointment at four o'clock. You want to leave early because class finishes at four o'clock. Ask your teacher.

   Can I leave class early? (OR: May I leave class early?)

2. You're in a friend's room. You're hot and you want to open the window. Ask your friend.

   _____

3. You're in an office. You want to use the telephone on the secretary's desk. Ask the secretary.

   _____

4. You're in your car and see a classmate at a bus stop. You want to give her a ride. Ask your classmate.

   _____

5. You're in class. You made a mistake, but you don't have an eraser. Your classmate has an eraser. Ask your classmate.

   _____

6. You're at your neighbor's house. You want to have a drink of water. Ask your neighbor.

   _____

7. You don't understand something in your grammar book. You want to ask your teacher a question.

   _____

8. You're at a restaurant. You want to sit at the empty table in the corner. Ask the waiter.

   _____

E DESIRES, INVITATIONS, AND POLITE REQUESTS: *WOULD LIKE, WOULD YOU LIKE, WOULD YOU PLEASE, COULD YOU PLEASE*

E.1

Read the conversations. Then answer the questions.

CONVERSATION A

A: Can I help you?

B: Yes, I'd like two tickets to Pittsburgh.

A: Would you like one-way or round-trip?

B: Round-trip, please.

A: That's $38.90.

B: Here you are. What time is the next bus?

A: At 9:30.

B: Thank you.

CONVERSATION B

A: Sir, would you like chicken or fish?

B: Chicken, please.

A: And what would you like to drink?

B: Just some water, please.

A: And your wife?

B: She doesn't want anything. She doesn't like airplane food.

CONVERSATION C

A: Where would you like to sit?

B: These seats are fine. I don't want to sit too close to the screen.

A: Would you like some popcorn?

B: No, but I'd like something to drink. But hurry! The movie's going to start.

1. Where does conversation A take place?   _____

2. Where does conversation B take place?   _____

3. Where does conversation C take place?   _____

E.2

Rewrite the sentences. Use **would like**.

1. I want two airmail stamps.

   I would like two airmail stamps. _____

2. Do you want to have dinner with me?

   _____

3. Sheila wants to talk to you.

   _____

4. Do your parents want to come?

   _____

5. Sandy and Billy want some coffee.

   _____

6. Does Dan want to come with us?

   _____

7. My friend and I want a table for two.

   _____

8. Does the teacher want to come to the party?

   _____

9. I want to take a long trip.

   _____

10. We want you to have dinner with us.

    _____

E.3

*Ari is making plans for a surprise birthday party for his roommate, Tony. He needs help from his friends. Look at his list. Write sentences. Use **would like**.*

Surprise Birthday Party

1. Jerry — do some of the shopping

2. Conchita — bring the CDs

3. Irene and Amira — help with the cooking

4. Eric — bring his CD player

5. Harry, Mike, and Tom — move the furniture

6. Ellen — buy some ice cream

7. Victor — pick up the birthday cake

8. Carmen and Ted — keep Tony busy

9. Ratana — make the decorations

1. *Ari would like Jerry to do some of the shopping.*

2. _____

3. _____

4. _____

5. _____

6. _____

7. _____

8. _____

9. _____

E.4

Complete the conversation. Use the words in parentheses.

Dave: Hi, Ellen. Come on in.

Ellen: Hi, Dave. Thanks.

Dave: (you/ like) _____*Would you like*_____ some coffee?
1.

Ellen: Yes. That sounds good. (you/ like) _____ some help?
2.

Dave: No, it's ready. Here you are.

Ellen: Thanks.

Dave: (you/ like) _____ some cookies, too?
3.

Ellen: No, thanks, but I (like) _____ some sugar.
4.

Dave: Oh, sorry. I forgot. Here's the sugar.

Ellen: Boy, it's cold outside.

Dave: (you/ like/me/give) _____ you a sweater?
5.

Ellen: No, I'm okay.

Dave: So, (what/ you/ like/ do) _____ this evening?
6.

Ellen: I don't know. (Where/ you/ like/go) _____?
7.

Dave: (you/ like/go) _____ to the movies?
8.

Ellen: What's playing?

Dave: *Forever Love* is at the Rex. (you/ like/see) _____ that?
9.

Ellen: Okay. What time does it start?

Dave: We can go at six, eight, or ten.

Ellen: I don't care. (What time/ you/ like/go) _____?
10.

Dave: Eight is fine, but I (like/get) _____ something to eat before.
11.

Ellen: Okay. (Where/ you/ like/eat) _____?
12.

Dave: How about John's Pizzeria?

Ellen: That sounds good.

E.5

Write the correct question. Use **would you** *or* **could you**.

1. Ask a stranger on the bus to tell you the time.

   Would you please tell me the time? (OR: Could you please tell me the time?)

2. Ask a desk clerk at a hotel to give you the key to your room.

   _____

3. Ask your teacher to explain the meaning of the word *grateful*.

   _____

4. Ask the cashier at the store to give you change for a dollar.

   _____

5. Ask a stranger on the street to take a picture of you and your friends.

   _____

6. Ask a taxi driver to take you to the airport.

   _____

7. Ask a neighbor to help you with your suitcases.

   _____

8. Ask a salesperson at a store to show you the brown shoes in the window.

   _____

9. Ask the person in front of you at a basketball game to sit down.

   _____

A BE GOING TO FOR THE FUTURE

11

Future;
Modals:
May and Might

A.1

Rewrite the sentences. Replace the underlined part with another future time expression. Use **tonight** *or* **next, this,** *or* **tomorrow** *with* **week, month, morning, afternoon, night,** *or* **evening.**

(*It's eleven o'clock in the morning on Wednesday, July 3rd.*)

1. Keith is going to attend a meeting <u>in four hours</u>.

   Keith is going to attend a meeting this afternoon.

2. Keith and his girlfriend, Andrea, are going to visit a friend in the hospital <u>in eight hours</u>.

   _____

3. Andrea is going to go on vacation <u>in one month</u>.

   _____

4. Keith and his brother are going to play tennis <u>in twenty hours</u>.

   _____

5. Keith's brother is going to see the doctor <u>in one week</u>.

   _____

6. Keith is going to call his mother <u>in eleven hours</u>.

   _____

7. Keith and Andrea are going to go to the movies <u>in thirty-four hours</u>.

   _____

149

A.2

Rewrite the sentences. Replace the underlined part with another future time expression. Use **in**.

(It is ten o'clock in the morning on Friday, March 5th.)

1. Richard is going to have lunch <u>at two o'clock this afternoon</u>.

   Richard is going to have lunch in four hours.

2. Richard and Irene are going to see his parents <u>on March 19th</u>.

   _____

3. Irene is going to get a haircut <u>on Monday, March 8th</u>.

   _____

4. Richard is going to graduate from college <u>on May 5th</u>.

   _____

5. Irene is going to arrive at Richard's house <u>at 10:10 this morning</u>.

   _____

A.3

What are your plans for tomorrow? Put a check (✓) next to the things you are probably going to do. Put an **X** *next to the things you are definitely not going to do.*

1. study _____

2. go shopping _____

3. clean _____

4. watch TV _____

5. go out with friends _____

6. listen to music _____

7. visit relatives _____

8. talk on the telephone _____

9. take a shower _____

10. write a letter _____

11. read a newspaper _____

12. stay home _____

A.4

Write six sentences about your plans for tomorrow. Use the information in exercise A.3.

Example: study   __✓__   write a letter   __X__

I am going to study tomorrow.

I am not going to write a letter.

1. _____
2. _____
3. _____
4. _____
5. _____
6. _____

A.5

Some people are going on vacation. Answer the questions about them. Use **be going to**.

These are some things Nina is taking:	These are some things Mr. and Mrs. Wu are taking:	These are some things Andy is taking:
a guidebook	fishing rods	a camera
a tennis racket	bicycles	skis
a bathing suit	paper and envelopes	books
		a guitar

A. What's Nina going to do on her vacation?

1. *She's going to go sightseeing.* _____

2. _____

3. _____

B. What are Mr. and Mrs. Wu going to do on their vacation?

4. _____

5. _____

6. _____

(Continued on next page.)

C. What's Andy going to do on his vacation?

7. _____

8. _____

9. _____

10. _____

A.6

Write sentences about the future. Use **be going to**.

1. It's Wednesday morning. Reggie usually plays tennis on Wednesday afternoon, but he has a bad cold.

   _____*He isn't going to play*_____ tennis this afternoon.

2. It's July. Joan usually takes a vacation in August, but she has money problems this year.

   _____ a vacation this August.

3. Mary always takes a shower in the morning, but there's no hot water today.

   _____ a shower this morning.

4. It's eleven o'clock in the morning. The children usually play outside after lunch, but the weather is terrible today.

   _____ outside this afternoon.

5. It's six o'clock. Carl and his wife usually watch television after dinner, but there's nothing good on television.

   _____ television tonight.

6. It's eleven o'clock. I usually have lunch around noon, but I finished a big breakfast at 10:30.

   _____ lunch at noon today.

7. It's twelve noon. My friend and I like to go swimming on Saturday afternoons, but my friend went away for the weekend and I'm tired.

   _____ swimming this afternoon.

8. It's nine o'clock in the morning. Dr. Morita usually sees patients at his office every morning, but there's a serious problem at the hospital. He can't leave until noon.

   _____ patients at his office this morning.

9. I usually wake up at six o'clock in the morning, but tomorrow is a holiday.

_____ at six o'clock tomorrow morning.

10. It's ten o'clock in the morning. The letter carrier usually delivers all the mail by one o'clock, but he

started late this morning.

_____ all the mail by one o'clock today.

A.7

Write questions. Use **be going to**.

1. What/he/make

   What is he going to make?

2. Who/cook/tonight

   _____

3. When/dinner/be/ready

   _____

4. Why/he/cook/so much food

   _____

5. How long/he/need/to cook the dinner

   _____

6. Who/come

   _____

7. How/he/cook/the lamb

   _____

8. Where/all of your guests/sit

   _____

9. What/you/do

   _____

10. How long/your guests/stay

    _____

A.8

Here are the answers to the questions in exercise A.7. Write each question in the correct blank.

1. **A:** _Who's going to cook tonight?_____

   B: My husband.

2. **A:** _____

   B: Soup, salad, lamb, potatoes, some vegetables, and dessert.

3. **A:** _____

   B: We're going to have a dinner party.

4. **A:** _____

   B: He's going to roast it in the oven.

5. **A:** _____

   B: About fifteen of my relatives.

6. **A:** _____

   B: My husband's fast. Probably two or three hours.

7. **A:** _____

   B: I'm going to wash the dishes.

8. **A:** _____

   B: At around seven o'clock.

9. **A:** _____

   B: They're going to come at 6:00 and probably stay until about 11:00.

10. **A:** _____

    B: My sister's going to bring extra chairs.

B PRESENT PROGRESSIVE FOR THE FUTURE

B.1

Underline the verb in each sentence. Write **now** *if the speaker is talking about now. Write* **future** *if the speaker is talking about the future.*

1. What <u>are</u> you <u>doing</u> tomorrow morning?   *future*

2. What <u>are</u> you <u>doing</u>?   *now*

3. I'm doing a grammar exercise. _____

4. We're not going on vacation in July. _____

5. She's leaving in two hours. _____

6. Are you doing anything special? _____

7. Is the plumber coming soon? _____

8. The students are not listening. _____

9. Where are you going? _____

10. Why is he going to the doctor's office? _____

B.2

Roger and Helen are taking a trip to Great Britain. Here is their schedule. Write sentences. Use the present progressive.

May 8	6:00 P.M.	Meet your group at the airport
	7:30	Fly to London
May 9	6:45 A.M.	Arrive in London
May 9 and 10		Stay at the London Regency Hotel
May 9	2:00 P.M.	Visit Buckingham Palace
	4:30	Have tea at the Ritz Hotel
	7:30	Go to the theater
May 10	9:00 A.M.	Go on a tour of central London
	12:00 P.M.	Eat lunch at a typical English pub
May 11	8:00 A.M.	Leave for Scotland

1. *They are meeting their group at the airport at 6:00 P.M. on May 8.*

2. _____

(Continued on next page.)

3. _____

4. _____

5. _____

6. _____

7. _____

8. _____

9. _____

10. _____

B.3

Write questions. Use the present progressive.

1. you/go/to English class/tomorrow

   Are you going to English class tomorrow?

2. you/go/to the movies/this weekend

   _____

3. you/take a trip/next week

   _____

4. your friend/come over/to your place/in two hours

   _____

5. your classmates from English class/meet you/for lunch tomorrow afternoon

   _____

6. your mother/drive to work/tomorrow

   _____

7. your father/take an English class/next year

   _____

8. your neighbors/make a party/for you/this weekend

   _____

9. you and your friends/play cards/next Saturday

_____

10. your parents/have dinner/with your English teacher/the day after tomorrow

_____

B.4

Answer the questions in exercise B.3. Use short answers.

1. _____

2. _____

3. _____

4. _____

5. _____

6. _____

7. _____

8. _____

9. _____

10. _____

B.5

Ask Rosemary about her vacation plans. Write questions. Use a word from each column and the present progressive.

Why		stay
When		take
Where	you	go
Who		go with
How long		leave
What		drive
How		get there

1. *Where are you going?* _____

To Colorado.

2. _____

On September 16th.

(Continued on next page.)

3. _____

By car.

4. _____

We're going camping.

5. _____

Two weeks.

6. _____

Some friends from college.

7. _____

A tent, sleeping bags, and bikes.

C WILL FOR THE FUTURE

C.1

*Complete the conversations. Use **I'll** and the words in the box.*

buy you some	make you a sandwich	wash them
get you some water	close the window	drive you
turn on the air conditioner	get you some aspirin	help you

1. **A:** I'm cold.

   B: *I'll close the window.* _____

2. **A:** I'm thirsty.

   B: _____

3. **A:** I can't lift this box.

   B: _____

4. **A:** I need some stamps.

   B: _____

5. **A:** I'm hot.

   B: _____

6. **A:** I'm hungry.

   B: _____

7. **A:** I have a headache.

   B: _____

8. **A:** I'm late for class.

   B: _____

9. **A:** There are dirty dishes in the sink.

   B: _____

C.2

Write the sentences in full form.

1. She'll be happy to see you.　　*She will be happy to see you.*

2. It'll be sunny tomorrow.　　_____

3. They won't know the story.　　_____

4. It won't be easy.　　_____

5. We'll take you to Ottawa.　　_____

6. I won't stay there for a long time.　　_____

7. He'll tell you later.　　_____

C.3

Write the sentences with contractions.

1. We will meet you at 8:00.　　*We'll meet you at 8:00.*

2. He will not lose his job.　　_____

3. I will have a cup of coffee.　　_____

4. It will rain this evening.　　_____

5. She will not be happy.　　_____

6. They will have a good time.　　_____

7. You will not like it.　　_____

C.4

Complete the sentences. Choose the correct words.

1. **A:** What's the weather forecast for tomorrow?

   B: The newspaper says it _____*will snow*_____ .
   a. is snowing
   b. will snow

2. **A:** Where are you going with the soap and water?

   B: I _____ wash the car.
   a. am going to
   b. will

3. **A:** Do you see my umbrella?

   B: Yes, it's over there. I _____ get it for you.
   a. am going to
   b. will

4. **A:** Why is Myra so happy these days?

   B: She _____ get married.
   a. is going to
   b. will

5. **A:** Why _____ see that film?
   a. are you going to
   b. will you

   B: I heard it was good.

6. **A:** The dishwasher isn't working. I'm going to call the repairman.

   B: No, don't. I _____ it.
   a. am fixing
   b. will fix

7. **A:** I think men _____ dresses in the future.
   a. are wearing
   b. will wear

   B: You're crazy!

8. **A:** _____ anything this weekend?

    a. Are you doing

    b. Will you do

    B: I'm not sure yet. Why?

9. **A:** _____ everything by computer in fifty years?

    a. Are people buying

    b. Will people buy

    B: Maybe.

C.5

Write negative sentences with the same meaning.

1. The car will be small.

    The car won't be big.

2. I'll leave early.

    _____

3. It'll be cold.

    _____

4. Coffee will cost less.

    _____

5. The dishes will be clean.

    _____

6. We will come after seven o'clock.

    _____

7. Mr. and Mrs. McNamara will buy an old car.

    _____

8. I'll make a few eggs.

    _____

9. Valerie will win the game.

    _____

10. The parking lot will be empty.

    _____

C.6

A fortune teller is telling Mark about his future. Complete the conversation.
Use **will** *and the words in parentheses.*

Fortune teller: Your future (be) _____ a happy one.
                                               1.

Mark: (I/be) _____ rich?
                           2.

Fortune teller: Yes. You (marry) _____ a very rich woman.
                                             3.

Mark: Where (I/meet) _____ her?
                               4.

Fortune teller: That I can't tell you, but it (be) _____ love at first sight.
                                                             5.

Mark: (she/love) _____ me forever?
                               6.

Fortune teller: Forever.

Mark: When (we/meet) _____ ?
                                 7.

Fortune teller: Soon.

Mark: What about children?

Fortune teller: You (not have) _____ many children—just two, a boy and a
                                           8.

girl.

Mark: That's a good number. What else?

Fortune teller: You (be) _____ famous.
                                     9.

Mark: Really? Why (I/be) _____ famous?
                                       10.

Fortune teller: I'm not sure, but it (not be) _____ fun for you.
                                                         11.

People (bother) _____ you all the time.
                          12.

Mark: Oh! I (not like) _____ that. (our home/have)
                                   13.

_____ everything?
              14.

Fortune teller: Yes, everything.

Mark: Good. Then we (not leave) _____ it, and people
                                               15.

(not bother) _____ us.
                       16.

Fortune teller: But then you (become) _____ a prisoner in your own
17.

home. (that/make) _____ you happy?
18.

Mark: Oh, why isn't life perfect?

Fortune teller: That I cannot tell you.

D MODALS: **MAY** OR **MIGHT** FOR POSSIBILITY

D.1

Write **permission** *if the speaker is giving, refusing, or asking for permission.*
Write **possibility** *if the speaker is talking about possibilities.*

1. Don't call Carol. She may be asleep.   *possibility*

2. It's noisy outside. May I close the window?   *permission*

3. You may not talk during the test. _____

4. The government may raise taxes. _____

5. Lie down! You might feel better. _____

6. You may enter that room of the museum, but be careful. _____

7. Some of the students might not do the homework. _____

8. May my roommate come to the party, too? _____

9. The mailman is coming. There may be a letter for me. _____

10. Nobody may leave before eleven o'clock. _____

D.2

Rewrite the sentences. Use **may** *or* **might**.

1. Maybe it will snow.

   It may snow. (OR: It might snow.)

2. Perhaps we'll come by taxi.

_____

3. Perhaps he won't want to come.

_____

(Continued on next page.)

4. Maybe they'll study.

_____

5. Perhaps the store will be closed.

_____

6. Maybe she won't finish the work by Friday.

_____

7. Maybe the dog will die.

_____

8. Perhaps you won't like that kind of food.

_____

9. Maybe I won't leave before seven o'clock.

_____

10. Perhaps the cookies won't taste good.

_____

D.3

Complete the sentences. Use **may** *or* **will**.

1. Tomorrow is my birthday. I _____*will*_____ be twenty-five.

2. I'm tall. My children _____*may*_____ be tall, too.

3. I don't know anything about that movie. It _____ not be any good.

4. Are you taking a trip to the United States? You _____ need a passport. Everybody from Brazil needs one.

5. Don't worry. I _____ do it. I promise.

6. Ask about the price. The picture _____ be expensive.

7. The supermarket _____ sell flowers, but I'm not sure.

8. There's someone at the door. I _____ open it.

9. The sun _____ rise tomorrow.

10. The food _____ be ready. I'm going to look.

D.4

Complete the sentences. Use **may (not)** *or* **might (not)** *and the words in the box.*

bite	close	get lost	have an accident	pass
break	fall	get sick	live	win

1. Janet is worried about her little boy. He's climbing a tree.

   He _may fall (OR: He might fall)._

2. Jimmy has a test today, and he didn't study.

   He _____

3. Lynn is driving fast.

   She _____

4. Wrap those glasses carefully.

   They _____

5. Mark Muller is one of the top tennis players in the world, but he isn't playing well today.

   He _____

6. Don't lose these directions. It's difficult to find my house.

   You _____

7. The woman's injuries are very bad.

   She _____

8. Don't go near that animal.

   It _____

9. Don't go outside with wet hair. It's cold.

   You _____

10. That store never has many customers.

    It _____

12

Comparisons

A COMPARATIVE FORM OF ADJECTIVES

A.1

Put a check (✓) next to the statements that are true.

1. Carol is neater than Yoko is.
2. Lulu is older than Pete is.
3. Doug is younger than Carol is.
4. Carol is more hardworking than Norma is.
5. Yoko is more interested in her studies than Carol is.
6. Lulu is busier than Pete is.
7. Yoko is farther from home than Carol is.

A.2

Put the words in the box in the correct column.

big	difficult	heavy	messy
careful	easy	high	noisy
comfortable	expensive	hot	old
crowded	fast	intelligent	pretty
dangerous	friendly	long	small

WORDS WITH ONE SYLLABLE	WORDS WITH TWO SYLLABLES	WORDS WITH THREE OR FOUR SYLLABLES
big	*careful*	*comfortable*

A.3

Complete the sentences. Use the comparative form of the adjectives.

1. That car is old, but this car is _____*older*_____ .
2. That book is good, but this book is ___better___ .

3. The train station is far, but the airport is ___farther___.

4. The student in the front is intelligent, but the student in the back is ___more inteligent___

5. The service at that restaurant is bad, but the food is ___worse___.

6. My sister's messy, but my brother is ___messier___.

7. This chair is comfortable, but that chair is ___more comfortable___.

8. My husband is careful, but his father is ___more carefuly___

9. The singer is pretty, but the actress is ___prettier___.

10. Chemistry is difficult, but physics is ___more difficult___

11. This unit's easy, but the last unit was ___easier___.

A.4

Complete the sentences. Use the comparative form of the adjectives in parentheses and **than**.

1. San Francisco is ___smaller than___ New York.
   (big, small)

2. The Nile River is ___longer than___ the Mississippi River.
   (long, short)

3. A Mercedes is ___more expensive than___ a Volkswagen.
   (cheap, expensive)

4. Mexico City is ___biger than___ Rome.
   (big, small)

5. The Himalayan Mountains are ___higher than___ the Rocky Mountains.
   (low, high)

6. Egypt is ___hotter than___ Canada.
   (cold, hot)

7. Skiing is ___more daugerous___ golf.
   (safe, dangerous)

8. Cities are ___more crowdeder than___ villages.
   (crowded, empty)

(Continued on next page.)

9. Cars are _noisier than_ bicycles.
               (noisy, quiet)

10. A rock is _heavier than_ a leaf.
               (heavy, light)

11. Cheetahs are _faster than_ monkeys.
               (slow, fast)

12. Dogs are _friendlier than_ wolves.
               (friendly, unfriendly)

A.5

Write questions. Use the comparative form of the adjectives.

    Example: Carol/neat/or/messy/Yoko

         Is Carol neater or messier than Yoko?

1. this unit/easy/or/difficult/the last unit

   Is this unit easier or more difficult than the las unit?

2. this workbook/cheap/or/expensive/the grammar book

   Is this workbook cheaper or more expensive than the grammar book?

3. you/young/or/old/your best friend

   are you younger or older than your best friend?

4. you/tall/or/short/your teacher

   are you taller or shorter than your teacher

5. your hometown/big/or/small/Los Angeles

   Is your hometown bigger or smaller than Los Angeles?

6. the weather today/good/or/bad/the weather yesterday

   Is the weather today better or worse than the weather yesterday

A.6

Answer the questions in exercise A.5.

Example: (Is Carol neater or messier than Yoko?)

Carol is messier.

1. _Unit is easier_
this 2. _Workbook is cheaper_
3. _I am younger_
4. _I am taller_
5. _____
6. _the weather today is better than the weather yesterday was._

B ADVERBS OF MANNER; COMPARATIVE FORM OF ADVERBS

taste
appear
become } estos no
seem } lloван
feel
look } LY
smell
sound

B.1

*Write **adjective** if the underlined word is an adjective. Write **adverb** if the underlined word is an adverb.*

1. Norma works hard. — _adverb_
2. Carol's room is dirty. — _adjective_
3. Pete drives slowly. — _adverb_
4. This exercise isn't hard. — _adj._
5. Everyone's going to come early. — _adv._
6. Carol did badly on the test. — "
7. Don't drive fast. — "
8. The food smells good. — _adj._
9. That shirt is ugly. — _adj._
10. I want to speak English fluently. — _adv._

Linking verbs are followed by adjective not adverbs

(Continued on next page.)

11. Carry these glasses <u>carefully</u>. _____*adv.*_____

12. I was <u>tired</u> yesterday. _____"_____

B.2

Find the ten adverbs in the box.

B	(H	A	P	P	I	L	Y)	F	X	X	X
A	E	A	S	I	L	Y	Q	A	X	X	X
D	A	N	G	E	R	O	U	S	L	Y	X
L	V	G	X	X	X	X	I	T	X	X	X
Y	I	R	P	A	T	I	E	N	T	L	Y
X	L	I	X	X	X	X	T	X	X	X	X
X	Y	L	X	W	E	L	L	X	X	X	X
X	X	Y	X	X	X	X	Y	X	X	X	X

B.3

Complete the sentences. Use the adverbs in exercise B.2.

1. It's snowing ____*heavily*____ . We can't drive in this weather.

2. Please play _____ . The baby's sleeping.

3. Vinny drives _____ . One day he's going to have an accident.

4. Lenore was an hour late for class. Her teacher looked at her _____ .

5. The children opened their Christmas presents _____ .

6. She plays the guitar very _____ . Everyone loves to listen to her.

7. I never eat my father's food. He cooks _____ .

8. I can't understand him. He speaks _____ .

9. I waited _____ , but the doctor never came.

10. I didn't get lost. I found the restaurant _____ .

B.4

Complete the sentences. Use the adjectives in the box in some sentences. In other sentences, use the adverb form of an adjective in the box.

angry	easy	loud
beautiful	fast	quiet
careful	good	tired

1. **A:** Shh! Be _____ *quiet* _____ ! The baby's sleeping.

   B: Okay. I'll open the door _____ *quietly* _____ .

2. **A:** The flowers are _____ .

   B: They smell _____ , too.

3. **A:** Is Gerry a _____ eater?

   B: Yes, she eats very _____. She always finishes dinner before me.

4. **A:** You look _____ .

   B: I am _____. I'm going to bed.

5. **A:** Did Samara do _____ on the test?

   B: Yes. She got an A. She's a _____ student.

6. **A:** Does your daughter drive _____ ?

   B: Oh, yes. She's a very _____ driver. I never worry about her.

7. **A:** The music in that apartment is always _____ .

   B: You're right. They play their music _____ . It's awful.

8. **A:** Why did she leave the room so _____ ?

   B: I'm not sure. I think she was _____ with her boss.

9. **A:** That was an _____ test.

   B: I agree. I answered all the questions very _____ .

B.5

Complete the sentences. Use the comparative form of the adverb.

1. **A:** Did Ruben come early?

   B: Yes, but I came _____*earlier*_____ .

2. **A:** Does Alejandro work hard?

   B: Yes, but En Mi works _____ .

3. **A:** Did your team play well?

   B: Yes, but the other team played _____ .

4. **A:** Does Andrew type carefully?

   B: Yes, but Brian types _____ .

5. **A:** Did the waiter yesterday serve you fast?

   B: Yes, but the waiter last week served us _____ .

6. **A:** Does Adam write neatly?

   B: Yes, but his sister writes _____ .

7. **A:** Does your husband dance badly?

   B: Yes, but I dance _____ .

8. **A:** Does the mechanic on Elm Street fix cars quickly?

   B: Yes, but the mechanic on Diamond Street fixes them _____ .

9. **A:** Did you learn to ride a bike easily?

   B: Yes, but my younger brother learned _____ .

10. **A:** Can you jump high?

    B: Yes, but Charlie can jump _____ .

11. **A:** Did the cashier speak to you rudely?

    B: Yes, but the manager spoke to me _____ .

C ADJECTIVE + ENOUGH;
TOO + ADJECTIVE;
VERY + ADJECTIVE

C.1

Match the questions and answers.

1. _b_ What's wrong with the soup?

2. ____ Do you want to go to that restaurant?

3. ____ Can you hear the music?

4. ____ Why are the other boys playing

   baseball without you?

5. ____ Do you like boxing?

6. ____ Are you going to wear that dress?

7. ____ Do you drive?

8. ____ Are you happy with your grade

   on the test?

a. No, it's too violent.

b. It's too salty.

c. I'm not good enough.

d. No, it's too tight.

e. No, I'm not old enough.

f. No, it's too crowded.

g. No, it isn't high enough.

h. No, the radio's not loud enough.

C.2

Rewrite the sentences. Use **too**.

1. The bathing suit isn't dry enough for me to wear.

   The bathing suit is too wet for me to wear.

2. The apartment isn't big enough for six people.

3. Shirley and Jack aren't fast enough to run in the race.

4. The car isn't cheap enough for us to buy.

(Continued on next page.)

5. The children aren't old enough to start school.

_____

6. The room isn't warm enough.

_____

C.3

Rewrite the sentences. Use **enough**.

1. It's too cold to sit outside.

  It isn't warm enough to sit outside.

2. The jacket is too small for me.

_____

3. The break was too short.

_____

4. It's too dark to take a picture.

_____

5. It's too noisy to talk.

_____

6. Buses are too slow.

_____

C.4

Complete the sentences. Use **too** *or* **very**.

1. **A:** Do you like my new dress?

   B: Yes, it's _____ pretty.

2. **A:** Put these sweaters in the drawer.

   B: I can't. The drawer's _____ full.

3. **A:** Mommy, I want to swim in the baby pool.

   B: You're _____ big. You're not a baby.

4. **A:** What do you think of that hotel?

   B: The rooms are _____ nice, but it's expensive.

5. **A:** How's the weather in Montreal in January?

   B: It's _____ cold.

6. **A:** Can you read that sign?

   B: No, it's _____ far away.

7. **A:** Are you going to buy the stereo?

   B: I think so. The price is _____ good.

8. **A:** The floor's _____ dirty.

   B: I'll wash it.

9. **A:** Put this bag in your pocket.

   B: I can't. It's _____ big.

C.5

Write one sentence from the two sentences.

1. I can't watch the movie. It's too sad.

   The movie is too sad for me to watch.

2. I can't drink this coffee. It's too strong.

   _____

3. Pete did not understand the instructions. They were too difficult.

   _____

4. We can't eat the fruit. It's not ripe enough.

   _____

5. We can't wait. The line's too long.

   _____

6. She didn't wash the sweater by hand. It was too dirty.

   _____

7. You can't marry him. He's not rich enough.

   _____

8. You can eat the eggs. They're cooked enough.

   _____

C.6

Complete the sentences. Use **enough** *or* **too** *and the adjective in parentheses.*

1. **A:** Why did you take the pants back to the store?

   B: They were (long) _____*too long*_____ . I exchanged them for a shorter pair.

2. **A:** Do you want me to wash the car again?

   B: Yes. It's (clean) _____*not clean enough*_____ .

3. **A:** Let's go into that big old house. I want to see what's in there.

   B: No, I don't want to. I'm (frightened) _____ . There may be ghosts.

4. **A:** Are the shoes comfortable?

   B: No, they're (big) _____ . I need a size 8, and they're a size 7.

5. **A:** Why didn't you get the tickets?

   B: It was (late) _____ . There weren't any left yet.

6. **A:** Is the soup okay?

   B: Yeah. Now it's (hot) _____ . Thanks for heating it up.

7. **A:** I'm going to go on a diet.

   B: Why? Are all your clothes (tight) _____ ?

8. **A:** Why do I need to write this composition again?

   B: Because it's (short) _____ . You wrote only 150 words, and I told

   you to write at least 250 words.

9. **A:** Can I borrow your bike?

   B: No, I'm sorry, but there's something wrong with the brakes. It's (safe)

   _____ to ride.

10. **A:** Dad, can we go in the water now?

    B: I don't know. It was cold before. Put your toe in the water and see if it's (warm)

    _____ now.

11. **A:** Why aren't the plants in the living room growing?

    B: Probably because it's (sunny) _____ . They need more light.

D AS + ADJECTIVE/ADVERB + AS;
THE SAME + NOUN + AS;
THE SAME AS;
DIFFERENT FROM

D.1

Put a check (✓) next to the sentences that are true.

1. Canada is the same size as the United States.

2. Lions are not as big as elephants.

3. 32° F is the same as 0° C.

4. The Statue of Liberty in New York is not as old as the Pyramids in Egypt.

5. Alaska is as cold as Antarctica.

6. A whale is different from a fish.

7. The British flag has the same colors as the American flag.

8. Silver is as valuable as gold.

D.2

Complete the sentences. Use **as** *or* **than**.

1. Russia is bigger _____*than*_____ the United States.

2. Is your classroom the same size _____*as*_____ the other classrooms?

3. South America is not as big _____ Asia.

4. English is more difficult _____ my native language.

5. The president of the United States is not the same age _____ the leader of my country.

6. I'm more tired today _____ I was yesterday.

7. Are doctors as rich _____ lawyers?

8. Are you as thin _____ your best friend?

9. Thelma's the same height _____ her brother.

10. Are animals more intelligent _____ human beings?

11. This book is better _____ that one.

12. Some people are friendlier _____ others.

D.3

Write sentences. Use the adjective in parentheses and **as . . . as** *or* **more . . . than**. *(Remember: = means* **equals***; < means* **less***; > means* **more***.)*

1. a Fiat < a Mercedes (expensive)

   A Fiat isn't as expensive as a Mercedes.

2. the book > the film (interesting)

   The book is more interesting than the film.

3. my apartment = your apartment (big)

   My apartment is as big as your apartment.

4. trains < airplanes (fast)

5. January = February (cold)

6. the chair = the sofa (comfortable)

7. the governor of Oregon < the president of the United States (famous)

8. the bank < the post office (far)

9. grapefruits = lemons (sour)

10. jazz > rock music (relaxing)

11. chocolate ice cream < vanilla ice cream (good)

12. some people > other people (violent)

13. college < high school (easy)

_____

14. these boxes = those boxes (heavy)

_____

D.4

Write questions. Use **the same** *and a word in the box.*

age	distance	color	height	length	price	size	weight

1. _Is your sister's hair the same color as your hair?_ _____

   No. My sister's hair is brown. My hair's black.

2. _____

   No. I'm 1.69 meters tall. My brother's 1.78 meters tall.

3. _____

   No. My mother's fifty-nine years old. My father's sixty-two.

4. _____

   No. The dining room's smaller than the living room.

5. _____

   Yes. The apples and the oranges are both sixty cents a pound.

6. _____

   No. I'm thinner than my brother.

7. _____

   No. *War and Peace* is over a thousand pages long. *Crime and Punishment* is much shorter.

8. _____

   No. The subway station is farther than the bus stop.

D.5

Write sentences. Use **the same as** *or* **different from**.

1. a wife and a housewife

   A wife is different from a housewife.

2. the U.S.A. and the United States

   The U.S.A. is the same as the United States.

3. a bike and a bicycle

   _____

4. a TV and a television

   _____

5. North America and the United States

   _____

6. 10,362 and 10.362

   _____

7. 3×16 and 16×3

   _____

8. $16 \div 3$ and $3 \div 16$

   _____

9. $1 and £1

   _____

10. a snack bar and a restaurant

    _____

11. 12:00 P.M. and noon

    _____

12. a plane and an airplane

    _____

E MORE/LESS/FEWER + NOUN; COMPARATIVE FORM OF ADJECTIVE + NOUN

E.1

Complete the sentences. Choose the correct word.

1. Alaska has _____ snow than Texas.
   a. more
   b. less

2. North America has _____ countries than Europe.
   a. more
   b. fewer

3. Small towns have _____ traffic than big cities.
   a. more
   b. less

4. There are _____ car accidents than train accidents.
   a. more
   b. fewer

5. Young people have _____ health problems than old people.
   a. more
   b. fewer

6. Germany has _____ oil than Iran.
   a. more
   b. less

7. Deserts have _____ rain than jungles.
   a. more
   b. less

8. Honolulu has _____ people than New York.
   a. more
   b. fewer

E.2

Write the words in the box in the correct column.

bedrooms	furniture
brothers	homework
cars	hours
children	jewelry
coffee	meat
courses	mistakes
food	money
free time	pairs of shoes
friends	traffic
fruit	women

FEWER	LESS
bedrooms	*jewelry*

E.3

Write sentences. Use **more . . . than**, **less . . . than**, *and* **fewer . . . than**.

1. Gail has five friends. Noah has fifteen friends.

   Gail *has fewer friends than Noah.*

2. Gail doesn't eat much fruit. Noah eats a lot of fruit every day.

   Gail *eats less fruit than Noah.*

3. Gail has three hours of homework every day. Noah has two hours of homework every day.

   Gail *has more homework than Noah.*

4. Gail has two brothers. Noah has one brother.

   Gail _____

5. Gail works twenty hours a week. Noah works thirty hours a week.

   Gail _____

6. Gail makes $5.50 an hour. Noah makes $7.15 an hour.

   Gail _____

7. Gail is taking five courses this semester. Noah is taking four courses.

   Gail _____

8. Gail drinks one cup of coffee a day. Noah drinks four cups of coffee a day.

   Gail _____

9. Gail's house has five bedrooms. Noah's house has three bedrooms.

   Gail's house _____

10. Gail has a little free time. Noah has a lot of free time.

    Gail _____

11. Gail has eight pairs of shoes. Noah has ten pairs of shoes.

    Gail _____

12. Gail eats meat once or twice a month. Noah eats meat every day.

    Gail _____

13. Gail's family has three cars. Noah's family has two cars.

    Gail's family _____

14. Gail's brother has two children. Noah's brother has one child.

    Gail's brother _____

15. Gail made two mistakes on last week's test. Noah made eight mistakes.

    Gail _____

E.4

Write sentences.

1. longer/my sister/I/hair/than/have

   I have longer hair than my sister.

2. Joanne/Steve and Harry/student/than/better/a/is

   Joanne, is a better student than Steve + Harry

3. serious/the other two salesmen/Mr. Page/than/makes/more/mistakes

   Mr. page makes more serious mistakes than the other salesmen.

4. the other ones/is/book/than/a/difficult/this/more

   this book is more difficult than the other ones.
   this is a more difficult book than the other ones.

5. a/kitchen/the apartments on the first floor/has/bigger/the apartment on the second floor/than

   the apartment on the second floor has a bigger kitchen than the apartment on the first floor.

(Continued on next page.)

6. more/secretaries/police officers/than/jobs/dangerous/have

Police officers _____ *have more dangerous jobs than secretaries*

7. than/bigger/Spain/India/population/a/has

India has a bigger population than Spain has

E.5

*Compare big cities and small towns. Use words from each column. (Don't forget! Add **a** where necessary.)*

		clean air	
		crowded streets	
		exciting night life	
A big city	usually has	friendly people	a small town
		large police department	
A small town		serious parking problems	a big city
		slow way of life	
		small public transportation system	

1. *A small town usually has cleaner air than a big city.* _____

2. _____

3. _____

4. _____

5. _____

6. _____

7. _____

8. _____

A PAST PROGRESSIVE:
AFFIRMATIVE AND NEGATIVE STATEMENTS, *YES/NO* QUESTIONS AND ANSWERS, *WH-* QUESTIONS

A.1

Put a check (✓) next to the sentences that are true.

1. I was sleeping at six o'clock yesterday morning.

2. While I was having dinner last night, the telephone rang.

3. This time last year I was not studying English.

4. I was walking down the street one day last week when I saw a friend.

5. My classmates and I were not taking a test at this time last week.

6. While I was getting dressed yesterday, birds were singing outside my window.

7. My family and I were watching TV at 9:30 last night.

8. While I was doing my homework the other day, I made some mistakes.

A.2

Complete the sentences. Use the words in the box and the past progressive.

buy some groceries	take a shower
cook dinner	talk on the phone
get gas	type
go to school	wait for the bus
study	wait in line

1. I saw Lulu and Bertha at the bus stop.

   They were waiting for the bus.

2. I called Lulu yesterday, but her line was busy.

   _____

(Continued on next page.)

3. I saw Uncle Bob and Aunt Valerie at the Hillside Restaurant.

_____

4. I saw Carol and Yoko at the library last night.

_____

5. I saw Pete's new secretary in the office.

_____

6. I saw Pete at the supermarket.

_____

7. When I called Elenore, she was in the bathroom.

_____

8. When I arrived at Norma's apartment, she was in the kitchen.

_____

9. When I went to the gas station, Milt was there.

_____

10. I saw Doug on 82nd Street.

_____

A.3

Write affirmative or negative sentences about the picture on page 63. Use the past progressive.

1. When I saw Doug at the fruit store, he (stand) _____*was standing*_____ in line.

2. When I saw Doug at the fruit store, he (eat) _____*wasn't eating*_____ an apple.

3. When I saw Doug at the fruit store, he (read) _____ .

4. When I saw Doug at the fruit store, three other people (wait) _____ in line.

5. When I saw Doug at the fruit store, the other people (stand) _____ in front of him.

6. When I saw Doug at the fruit store, he (wear) _____ pants.

7. When I saw Doug at the fruit store, he (hold) _____ his history book.

8. When I saw Doug at the fruit store, he (buy) _____ bananas.

9. When I saw Doug at the fruit store, the other customers (leave) _____ .

A.4

Write sentences. Use the past progressive and the simple past in each sentence.

1. When/the teacher/ask/me a question/I/read

   When the teacher asked me a question, I was reading.

2. While/my father/talk/to me/someone/ring/the doorbell

   _____

3. The boys/play/basketball/when/the fight/start

   _____

4. I/swim/when/I/get/a pain in my leg

   _____

5. When/we/see/the accident/we/drive/down Market Street

   _____

6. The doctor/examine/Mrs. May/when/she/scream

   _____

7. While/I/wash/my hair/I/get/some soap in my eyes

   _____

8. Alan/shave/when/he/cut/himself

   _____

9. The train/come/while/we/get/our tickets

   _____

A.5

Write questions. Use the past progressive.

1. **A:** Simon and Barbara have breakfast between 7:00 and 7:30 every morning.

   B: _Were they having breakfast_ _____ yesterday morning at 7:15?

   A: I think so.

2. **A:** Simon meets with his salespeople every morning between 9:00 and 9:30.

   B: _____ at 9:20 yesterday morning?

   A: Probably.

3. **A:** Barbara teaches every day between one o'clock and four o'clock.

   B: _____ yesterday at three o'clock?

   A: Of course.

4. **A:** Simon swims every Monday and Wednesday between noon and 12:45.

   B: _____ last Wednesday at 12:30?

   A: Probably.

5. **A:** Barbara practices the piano every morning between 9:00 and 10:00.

   B: _____ at 9:30 yesterday morning?

   A: Almost definitely.

6. **A:** Simon listens to a business report on the radio every afternoon between 4:30 and 5:00.

   B: _____ at 4:45 yesterday afternoon?

   A: I guess so.

7. **A:** Simon and Barbara have dinner between six o'clock and seven o'clock.

   B: _____ at 6:30 yesterday?

   A: Yes.

8. **A:** Simon and Barbara watch the news every evening between 7:00 and 7:30.

   B: _____ yesterday evening at 7:15?

   A: I think so.

9. **A:** Barbara takes a bath every evening between 9:00 and 9:30.

   B: _____ at 9:15 yesterday evening?

   A: Probably.

A.6

Answer the questions. Use the simple past or the past progressive of the verbs in parentheses.

1a. **A:** What were you doing when it started to rain?

 B: We (have) _____ a picnic.

1b. **A:** What did you do when it started to rain?

 B: We (hurry) _____ to the car.

2a. **A:** What were you doing when the phone rang?

 B: I (watch) _____ TV.

2b. **A:** What did you do when the phone rang?

 B: I (answer) _____ it.

3a. **A:** What were the children doing when the fire started?

 B: They (sleep) _____ .

3b. **A:** What did the children do when the fire started?

 B: They (run) _____ out of the house.

4a. **A:** What were you doing when the teacher came in?

 B: We (stand) _____ around.

4b. **A:** What did you do when the teacher came in?

 B: We (sit) _____ down.

5a. **A:** What was Susan doing when she fell?

 B: She (climb) _____ a tree.

5b. **A:** What did Susan do when she fell?

 B: She (call) _____ her mother.

6a. **A:** What was your father doing when he burned his hand?

 B: He (iron) _____ .

6b. **A:** What did your father do when he burned his hand?

 B: He (put) _____ some ice on the burn.

A.7

Write questions. Use the verbs in the box and **how fast, what, when, where, who,** *or* **why**.

do	drive	go	ride	stand	wait

1. **A:** *Where were you standing* _____ when the accident happened?

   B: I was standing on the corner of Buick and 3rd Street.

2. **A:** _____ ?

   B: I was waiting.

3. **A:** _____ ?

   B: I was waiting for the bus.

4. **A:** _____ ?

   B: I was going to the gym.

5. **A:** _____ ?

   B: Because I always go to the gym on Mondays.

6. **A:** _____ the red car?

   B: A teenager was driving the red car.

7. **A:** _____ ?

   B: He was going at least 65 miles per hour.

8. **A:** _____ ?

   B: I don't know. Maybe he was driving so fast because the other person in the car was ill.

9. **A:** _____ in the car with him?

   B: An older woman. Maybe it was his mother.

B DIRECT AND INDIRECT OBJECTS

B.1

Who probably said each of the sentences? Match the sentences and speakers.

1. __f__ "Please show me your driver's license."

2. _____ "I'll explain the answers to you in the next class."

3. _____ "Would you cash this check for me?"

4. _____ "I can fix the car for you on Wednesday."

5. _____ "Please pass me the salt and pepper."

6. _____ "Sure. I'll lend you my car for the weekend."

7. _____ "I want to buy my mother something for her birthday."

8. _____ "We'll send the information to you right away."

9. _____ "Could you please give me your passport?"

a. an immigration officer

b. a mechanic

c. someone at a restaurant

d. someone at an office

e. a teacher

f. a police officer

g. a bank customer

h. a friend

i. a child

B.2

Write the direct object and indirect object in each sentence in exercise B.1.

	DIRECT OBJECT	INDIRECT OBJECT
1.	*your driver's license*	*me*
2.		
3.		
4.		
5.		
6.		
7.		
8.		
9.		

B.3

Stephen and Margo got married last month. They got many wedding presents. Complete the sentences. Put the direct object before the indirect object. Be sure to use the correct preposition.

Frank	some glasses
Kate	a silver bowl
Tim and June	a TV
Julie	a painting
Mike and Sally	some dishes
Robert	the wedding cake

1. Frank gave some *glasses to Stephen and Margo.* _____

2. Kate got _____

3. Tim and June bought _____

4. Julie sent _____

5. Mike and Sally gave _____

6. Robert made _____

B.4

Christmas is coming soon. Here are the presents Bernie is going to give. Complete the sentences. Put the indirect object before the direct object.

Lucy	a sweater
Bob	a CD
Bill	a book
Marge	some earrings
his brother	some pajamas
his cousin	some sunglasses

1. *He's going to give Lucy a sweater.* _____

2. _____

3. _____

4. _____

5. _____

6. _____

B.5

Complete the sentences. Use the correct preposition and **it, them, me, him,** *or* **her**.

1. This is Carol's book. Give _____ *it to her.* _____

2. This is Pete and Elenore's invitation. Send _____

3. These are Bertha's bananas. Give _____

4. Those are my keys. Hand _____

5. Norma wants those flowers. Buy _____

6. Uncle Bob and Aunt Valerie like that picture. Get _____

7. I want fried eggs. Make _____

8. I need the salt. Pass _____

9. Milt can't find his pen. Find _____

10. Bertha and Lulu want to see the newspaper. Show _____

B.6

Write sentences.

1. lent/him/some money/I.

   I lent him some money. _____

2. to/some money/I/him/lent.

   _____

3. me/pronounce/this/for/you/would?

   _____

4. the women/the man/something/is/to/showing.

   _____

5. them/you/some help/give/can?

   _____

6. you/tell/the answer/him/did?

   _____

7. these cookies/for/got/I/the children.

   _____

(Continued on next page.)

8. all my friends/birthday cards/I/send.

_____

9. fixed/me/Sharon/my watch/for.

_____

10. to/the ball/me/throw.

_____

11. this sentence/us/would/you/to/explain?

_____

12. me/he/fifty dollars/owes

_____

C *TOO/EITHER*

▼

C.1

Complete the sentences. Use **too** *or* **either.**

1. **A:** Simone doesn't speak English perfectly.

   B: I don't, _____*either*_____ .

2. **A:** Peter is eighteen years old.

   B: Fidel and Maria are, _____ .

3. **A:** Doctors study for many years.

   B: Dentists do, _____ .

4. **A:** Penny has two cats.

   B: Dana does, _____ .

5. **A:** We don't know the answer to the third question.

   B: I don't, _____ .

6. **A:** Helga can't ski very well.

   B: Paul can't, _____ .

7. **A:** John Kennedy died a long time ago.

   B: Martin Luther King did, _____ .

8. **A:** The cake won't be ready in half an hour.

   B: The pie won't, _____ .

9. **A:** The hamburger wasn't good.

   B: The french fries weren't, _____ .

C.2

Complete the sentences.

1. Carol goes to college in Oregon, and Yoko _____*does*_____ , too.

2. Doug's last name is Winston, and Norma's _____ , too.

3. Carol didn't clean up her room yesterday, and Doug _____ , either.

4. Carol has a lot of friends, and Yoko _____ , too.

5. Lulu has an apartment in Florida, and Bertha _____ , too.

6. Pete Winston wasn't home last night, and Elenore _____ , either.

7. Carol doesn't speak Japanese, and Lulu _____ , either.

8. Doug doesn't have a car, and Norma _____ , either.

9. Doug isn't a very good student, and Carol _____ , either.

10. Carol went to San Francisco for Thanksgiving, and Yoko _____ , too.

11. Carol can drive, and Yoko _____ , too.

12. Pete won't be late for work tomorrow, and his secretary _____ , either.

C.3

Complete the sentences. Use **too** *or* **either**.

> Hi! I'm Anne's mother.
> I can speak Spanish,
> but I can't speak German.
> I don't have much free time.

> Hi! I'm Anne's father.
> I have brown hair.
> I drive to work every day.
> I didn't go out last weekend.

> Hi! I'm Anne's sister.
> I'm not married.
> I'm going to Hawaii on vacation.
> I wasn't born in a hospital.

> Hi! I'm Anne's brother.
> I took piano lessons
> a long time ago.
> I don't know how to ski.
> I was a good student in college.

1. Anne doesn't know how to ski, *and her brother doesn't, either.* _____

2. Anne can speak Spanish, *and her mother can, too.* _____

3. Anne has brown hair, _____

4. Anne took piano lessons a long time ago, _____

5. Anne isn't married, _____

6. Anne didn't go out last weekend, _____

7. Anne was a good student in college, _____

8. Anne is going to Hawaii on vacation, _____

9. Anne wasn't born in a hospital, _____

10. Anne drives to work every day, _____

11. Anne can't speak German, _____

12. Anne doesn't have much free time, _____

D PHRASAL VERBS WITH DIRECT OBJECTS

D.1

Complete the sentences. Use **away, back, down, in, off,** *or* **on.**

1. I was hot, so I took _____*off*_____ my sweater.

2. I was cold, so I put _____ my jacket.

3. I put all the dishes in the dishwasher. Would you turn it _____ ?

4. Would you turn _____ the light? I want to go to sleep.

5. Time is up. Please hand _____ your test papers.

6. The weather is going to be bad tomorrow. Let's put _____ the picnic until next weekend.

7. The test is going to begin. Put all your books and notes _____ .

8. These clothes are too small for the baby now. Let's give them _____ .

9. I'm going to throw _____ yesterday's newspaper.

10. Can I give your umbrella _____ to you tomorrow? I need it today.

D.2

Rewrite the sentences in two different ways.

1. Turn on the TV.   *Turn the TV on.*   *Turn it on.*

2. I'll put away the food. _____ _____

3. I'll turn down the radio. _____ _____

4. Let's put off the meeting. _____ _____

5. Please hand out these papers. _____ _____

6. I threw away the wrong thing. _____ _____

7. Please take off your shoes. _____ _____

8. The store will not take back bathing suits. _____ _____

9. Turn off the engine. _____ _____

10. Don't put on any makeup. _____ _____

D.3

Answer the questions. Use a word from each column.

call		
give		away
look		back
put	it	off
take	them	on
throw		up
turn		

1. What do you do with your clothes before you go to bed?

   I *take them off.* _____

2. What do you do when you want to listen to the radio?

   I _____

3. What do you do with your alarm clock when it rings?

   I _____

4. What do you do with sour milk?

   I _____

5. What do you do with a pen after you borrow it?

   I _____

6. What do you do with your shoes before you leave home?

   I _____

7. What do you do with a stereo when it isn't loud enough?

   I _____

8. What do you do with the things on your bed when you want to go to sleep?

   I _____

9. What do you do when you don't know the meaning of a word?

   I _____

10. What do you do when you want to talk to your friends on the phone?

    I _____

E PHRASAL VERBS WITHOUT OBJECTS

E.1

Rewrite the sentences. Replace the underlined words. Use the phrasal verbs in the box.

break down	come in	hang up
catch on	eat out	show up
clear up		

1. Please <u>enter</u>.

   Please come in
   _____

2. We like to <u>eat in a restaurant</u>.

   _____

3. The weather will <u>get better</u>.

   _____

4. Some cars often <u>stop working</u>.

   _____

5. The taxi will <u>arrive</u> soon.

   _____

6. Don't <u>end the phone conversation</u>.

   _____

7. Short skirts will probably <u>become popular</u> again.

   _____

E.2

Add **it** *where necessary.*

1. **A:** I can't hear the music.
   B: I'll turn ∧*it* up.

2. **A:** Is this my hat?
   B: Yes. Put on.

3. **A:** Why are you walking?
   B: The elevator broke down.

4. **A:** Where's the bus?
   B: It always shows up late on Fridays.

5. **A:** Do you want this box?
   B: No. Throw away.

6. **A:** Is your father still on the phone?
   B: No. He hung up.

7. **A:** Do you want to eat home tonight?
   B: No. Let's eat out.

8. **A:** Are you finished with the iron?
   B: Yes. Could you turn off?

9. **A:** May I come in?
   B: Yes. Please sit down.

10. **A:** Where's your new CD player?
    B: It didn't work right, so I took back.

E.3

Complete the sentences. Use one word from each box.

ate	cleared	sat	stayed
broke	grew	showed	stood
came	hung	shut	woke

down	out
in	up

1. One of the students ___*stood up*___ and left the room.

2. I got the wrong number, so I _____ .

3. It was cloudy in the morning, but in the afternoon it _____ .

4. I live in Virginia now, but I _____ in Kansas. My parents still live there.

5. We _____ at the table and started to eat.

6. Our car _____ , so we called the mechanic.

7. I _____ late at the party, and there was no food left.

8. I didn't leave work on time because a problem _____ .

9. There was no food in the refrigerator, so we _____ last night.

10. Don't say, " _____ ." Say, "Be quiet." It's more polite.

11. I'm tired this morning because I _____ late last night.

12. I _____ in the middle of the night because I had a bad dream.

14

A SHOULD

A.1

Complete the sentences. Use **should** *or* **shouldn't**

1. Children _____*shouldn't*_____ play with matches.

2. Children _____ watch television all day long.

3. Children _____ listen to their parents.

4. Children _____ eat a lot of candy.

5. Children _____ play in the street.

6. Teenagers _____ pay attention in school.

7. Teenagers _____ keep their bedrooms neat.

8. Teenagers _____ stay out all night with their friends.

9. Adults _____ exercise at least twice a week.

10. Adults _____ drink ten cups of coffee a day.

A.2

Rewrite the sentences. Use **ought to**.

1. You should go to the dentist twice a year.

   You ought to go to the dentist twice a year.

2. I should visit my grandparents more often.

   _____

3. All passengers should arrive at the airport an hour before their flight.

   _____

4. Carol should study harder.

   _____

5. We should take something to the party.

   _____

A.3

Rewrite the sentences. Use **should**.

1. Carol ought to clean her room more often.

   Carol should clean her room more often.

2. You ought to cook the meat a little longer.

   _____

3. Lulu ought to be nicer to Elenore.

   _____

4. I ought to learn how to type.

   _____

5. Pete and Elenore ought to move into a smaller apartment.

   _____

A.4

Complete the sentences. Use **should** *or* **shouldn't** *and the words in the box.*

get a haircut	smoke
go to the dentist	study more
leave a tip	touch it
leave early	wash it
look for another one	watch it

1. You don't look very nice. You *should get a haircut.* _____

2. I don't like my job. I _____

3. John often has a bad cough. He _____

4. Myra has a toothache. She _____

5. The car is dirty. You _____

6. The waiter is terrible. We _____

7. Doug and Jason aren't doing well in math. They _____

8. There's going to be a lot of traffic. We _____

9. That movie is very violent. The children _____

10. That dog may bite. You _____

A.5

Complete the dialogue. Write questions with **should.** *Use* **what, who, when, why, how many,** *or* **where** *and the verbs in parentheses.*

A: Let's have a party.

B: Okay. (have) _____ *When should we have* _____ it?
   1.

A: Let's have it on March 23rd.

B: (have) _____ it then?
   2.

A: Because it's Lucy's birthday.

B: Oh, that's right. (invite) _____?
   3.

A: Probably around twenty-five people.

B: (invite) _____?
   4.

A: Let's see . . . the neighbors, Lucy's family, the people from the office.

B: (buy) _____ ?
   5.

A: Well, we'll need drinks, potato chips, and things like that.

B: (cook) _____ ?
   6.

A: I'll make some lasagna.

B: That sounds good, and I'll make some salad. (get) _____ a
   7.

birthday cake from?

A: I like the Savoy Bakery's cakes.

B: Okay. Let's order one from there.

A: You know, we don't have enough dishes and glasses for twenty-five people.

(do) _____ ?
   8.

B: That's no problem. We can get paper plates and cups at the supermarket.

A: You're right. That's a good idea. (send) _____ out the
   9.

invitations?

B: I'll write them this weekend.

B HAD BETTER

▼

B.1

Match the sentences and situations. Write the sentences in the correct boxes.

1. We'd better take a taxi.

2. We'd better ask for directions.

3. We'd better not stay up late.

4. We'd better make sure everything is locked.

5. We'd better look at a map.

6. We'd better not wait for the bus.

7. We'd better not stay in the sun anymore.

8. We'd better get a good night's sleep.

9. We'd better throw away the food in the refrigerator.

10. We'd better put some cream on our arms and legs.

a. We're lost	b. We're getting red	c. We're going to be late
		We'd better take a taxi.

d. We'll be away for three weeks	e. We have an exam tomorrow

B.2

Don and Amy are going to have a dinner party. Complete the sentences. Use **had better** *or* **had better not** *and the words in the box.*

ask Costas to bring her borrow some from the neighbors get a couple of bottles invite him	let the dog in the house make roast beef rent a video film serve shrimp sit together at the table

1. Alan can't eat meat.

   We _had better not make roast beef._

2. Marsha and Sophia don't like each other.

   They _____

3. Tonya has a new boyfriend.

   We _____

4. Joan doesn't like fish or seafood.

   We _____

5. Ed drinks only Diet Coke.

   We _____

6. Chris is allergic to animals.

   We _____

7. We don't have enough chairs.

   We _____

8. The children will probably get bored.

   We _____

9. Sandy doesn't drive, and she can't take a bus here.

   We _____

C HAVE TO, DON'T HAVE TO, MUST

C.1

Put a check (✓) next to the sentences that are true.

1. People in my country have to pay taxes.

2. People in my country don't have to vote.

3. Drivers in my country have to have driver's licenses.

4. Students in my country don't have to wear uniforms in high school.

5. Young people in my country don't have to do military service.

6. Women in my country had to obey their husbands many years ago.

7. Children in my country did not have to go to school many years ago.

8. Children in my country had to go to work at a young age many years ago.

C.2

Rewrite the sentences. Use **have to, has to, don't have to, doesn't have to, had to,** *or* **didn't have to.**

1. It's necessary for me to finish this exercise.

   I *have to finish this exercise.*

2. It isn't necessary for me to do the last exercise again.

   I _____ _____

3. It wasn't necessary for Doug to go to school yesterday.

   Doug _____

4. It was necessary for Carol to clean her room yesterday.

   Carol _____

5. It isn't necessary for Yoko to write her parents every week.

   Yoko _____

6. It wasn't necessary for Pete and Elenore to go shopping last week.

   Pete and Elenore _____

(Continued on next page.)

7. It's necessary for my classmates and me to take tests.

   My classmates and I _____

8. It isn't necessary for Pete and Elenore to buy a new car.

   Pete and Elenore _____

9. It's necessary for Lulu to see her doctor today.

   Lulu _____

10. It's necessary for me to check my answers to this exercise.

    I _____

C.3

Complete the sentences. Use **have to** *and* **don't have to** *in each sentence.*

1. Students _____*don't have to*_____ stay in school twelve hours a day, but they

   _____*have to*_____ study.

2. Teachers _____ correct papers, but they _____

   wear uniforms.

3. Police officers _____ speak a foreign language, but they

   _____ wear uniforms.

4. Doctors _____ study for many years, but they

   _____ know how to type.

5. Secretaries _____ work at night, but they _____

   know how to type.

6. Firefighters _____ work at night, but they _____

   study for many years.

7. Fashion models _____ work seven days a week, but they

   _____ worry about their appearance.

8. Farmers _____ get up early in the morning, but they

   _____ worry about their appearance.

9. Basketball players _____ practice regularly, but they

_____ play a game every day.

10. Accountants _____ be good writers, but they _____

be good with numbers.

C.4

Complete the sentences. Use **have to, has to, don't have to,** *or* **doesn't have to.**

1. **A:** Is Dan getting up early this morning?

   B: No, he _*doesn't have to get up early this morning.*_ There's no school.

2. **A:** Is Sheila leaving early today?

   B: Yes, she _____ She has a dentist appointment.

3. **A:** Are you going food shopping today?

   B: Yes, I _____ There's no food in the house.

4. **A:** Are you and your wife coming by taxi?

   B: Yes, we _____ Our car isn't working.

5. **A:** Is Barbara staying at the office late today?

   B: No, she _____ Her boss is on vacation.

6. **A:** Are the children cleaning up their room?

   B: No, they _____ I cleaned it up yesterday.

7. **A:** Is Mary taking some medicine?

   B: Yes, she _____ She has a stomach problem.

8. **A:** Are you paying for the tickets?

   B: No, we _____ They're free.

9. **A:** Is José going to wear a suit and tie this morning?

   B: Yes, he _____ He's going to an important business meeting.

10. **A:** Does Bonnie do housework?

    B: No, she _____ She has a maid.

C.5

Write sentences. Use **must** *or* **mustn't** *and the words in the box.*

drive faster than 55 mph enter go more slowly	make a U-turn park in this area pass	stop turn left turn right

1.

2.

3.

4.

5.

6.

7.

8.

9.

1. *You mustn't enter.* _____

2. _____

3. _____

4. _____

5. _____

6. _____

7. _____

8. _____

9. _____

C.6

Mr. and Mrs. Chung were on vacation last week. Write sentences. Use **had to** *or* **didn't have to.**

```
do anything special
find someone to take care of their dog
get to the airport on time
get up early every morning
go to work
look for a hotel
make the bed every morning
pack and unpack suitcases
pay their hotel bill
wash dishes
```

1. *They didn't have to do anything special.* _____

2. _____

3. _____

4. _____

5. _____

6. _____

7. _____

8. _____

9. _____

10. _____

C.7

Write questions.

1. have/English/in class/you/to/do/speak

   Do you have to speak English in class?
   _____

2. get up/to/your/have/does/in the morning/at 6:00/mother

   _____

3. you/to/last night/cook/did/have

   _____

(Continued on next page.)

4. best friend/do/does/to/have/your/this exercise

_____

5. to/you/on time/in/have/English class/do/be

_____

6. friends/learn/to/do/English/your/have

_____

7. shave/father/have/your/did/to/yesterday

_____

8. your/to work/to/best friend/yesterday/did/have/go

_____

9. a/to/test/you/have/did/last week/take

_____

C.8

Answer the questions in exercise C.7. Use short answers.

1. (Do you have to speak English in class?)

   Yes, we do. _____

2. _____

3. _____

4. _____

5. _____

6. _____

7. _____

8. _____

9. _____

C.9

Write questions. Use **have to**.

1. I have to buy some food.

   What *do you have to buy?* _____

2. She has to get a book from the library.

   Why _____

3. He has to go.

   Where _____

4. The teacher had to talk to someone.

   Who _____

5. We had to stay there a long time.

   How long _____

6. The students have to stay after class.

   Why _____

7. I have to use eggs.

   How many eggs _____

8. The high school students had to send their college applications.

   When _____

9. I have to get up early.

   What time _____

10. He had to borrow some money.

    How much money _____

D SUPERLATIVE FORM OF ADJECTIVES AND ADVERBS

D.1

Answer the questions about the Winston family. Write **Carol, Doug,** *or* **Norma.**

1. Who's the oldest? _____ *Norma* _____

2. Who's the youngest? _____

3. Who's the neatest? _____

4. Who lives the farthest from home? _____

5. Who's the most serious of the three? _____

6. Who has the busiest social life? _____

7. Who's most interested in fashionable clothes? _____

D.2

Complete the sentences. Use the superlative form of the adjective.

1. The kitchen is always hot. It's _____ *the hottest* _____ room in the house.

2. Roger's a bad student. He's _____ student in the class.

3. Chemistry is hard. For me, it's _____ subject in school.

4. Roses are beautiful flowers. In fact, many people think that roses are _____ flowers.

5. Noon is a busy time at the bank. In fact, it's _____ time.

6. "Married Young" is a funny program. It's _____ program on TV.

7. *Scully's* is a good restaurant. In fact, it's _____ restaurant in town.

8. I think monkeys are ugly. In my opinion, they're _____ animals in the zoo.

9. *Midnight* is a popular nightclub. It's _____ nightclub in town.

10. *Dixon's* has low prices. It has _____ prices in the neighborhood.

11. Pamela's a fast swimmer. She's _____ swimmer on the team.

12. Jake is charming. He's _____ person of all my friends.

D.3

Put the words in the correct order. Then write two sentences. Use the adjectives in parentheses.

1. a train/a plane/a bus   (fast)

   A plane is the fastest of the three.

   A train is faster than a bus.

2. a teenager/a child/a baby   (old)

   A teenager is the oldest of a baby a child

3. a Ford/a Rolls Royce/a BMW   (expensive)

   A Rolls Royce is the most expensive than a ford

4. Nigeria / Turkey/Sweden   (hot)

   Nigeria is the hottest of. Sweden

5. a street/a path/a highway   (wide)

   A highway is the widest of a street

6. a city/a village/a town   (big)

   A city is the biggest than of the two.

7. an elephant/a gorilla /a fox   (heavy)

   An Elephant is the heaviest of the tree

8. an hour/a second/a minute   (long)

   An hour is the longest of the three

(Continued on next page.)

9. boxing/golf/soccer   (dangerous)

Boxing is more dangeroos than soccer and golf.
Boxing is the most dangeroos of the three

10. a banana/a carrot/chocolate   (fattening)

Chocolate is the more fattening thanthe three

D.4

Write sentences. Use the superlative form of the adverbs in parentheses.

1. Andy came at 6:00. Mike came at 6:20. Jean came at 6:40.

   (late)   *Jean came the latest.*

   (early)   *Andy came the earliest*

2. The red car is going 50 miles per hour. The blue car is going 65 miles per hour. The white car's

   going 73 miles per hour.

   (slowly)   *the red car is going the slowliest of the three*

   (fast)   *the whitecar is the fastest of the three*

3. Shirley drives well and never has car accidents. Maurice usually drives well, but he had an

   accident last year. Fran drives badly; she had two accidents last year and one accident this year.

   (dangerously)   *Fran drives the most dangerously of the three.*

   (carefully)   *Shirley drives the most carefully of the three*

4. Gary works two miles from his home. Viv works fifteen miles from her home. Harris works thirty

   miles from his home.

   (close)   *Gary works the closest to his house*

   (far)   *Harris works the farthest from his house*

5. Milton speaks a few words of Spanish. Linda can speak Spanish, but she always makes mistakes.

   Carolyn speaks Spanish and never makes mistakes.

   (well)   *carolyn speaks spanish the best of the three*

   (badly)   *Milton speaks spanish the worst.*

6. Sam types fifty words a minute but always makes at least six mistakes. Joan types sixty words a minute but doesn't usually make any mistakes. Renée types seventy-five words a minute but often makes two or three mistakes.

(quickly) _____

(accurately) _____

A.1

Find the fourteen verb tense mistakes in the postcard.
Then correct them.

May 22nd

Dear Mom and Dad,

    Greetings from Venice. Dan and I ~~am~~ *are* fine. We have a wonderful time on our honeymoon. The weather isn't great, but Venice be such a romantic place. It have so many beautiful places.

    Yesterday we walk all around the city. We visit several churches. They was so wonderful, and we see so many gorgeous paintings.

    Today it rained all morning, so we didn't went far from our hotel. This afternoon we have lunch at a very good restaurant across from the hotel. We both eat special Venetian dishes and enjoyed them very much.

    It is five o'clock now, and Dan rests. Tonight after dinner—maybe we'll go to a pizzeria—we take a gondola ride. I can't wait!

        Love,
        Carol

TO: Pete and Elenore Winston
     4526 Riverside Drive
     New York, NY 10027

A.2

Read Carol's diary. Then write questions. Use **who,**
where, when, what, what time, how long, *or* **why.**

May 20th

Venice is such a wonderful place. We arrived at eleven o'clock this morning, and I already love it. I still can't believe it, but we took a boat from the airport to our hotel on the Grand Canal. Tonight we're going to take a gondola ride.

1. *When did they arrive in Venice?*

   At eleven o'clock on May 20th.

2. _____

   It's on the Grand Canal.

3. _____

   They're going to take a gondola ride.

May 21st

Well, it rained all night last night, so we stayed in our hotel. I really wanted to go on the gondola ride, but it was impossible in the rain.

Today we're going on a walking tour of the city. The tour will start at 9:00. (It's 7:30 now, and Dan is sleeping.) The tour guide is a professor of art history at the university here. I think it will be interesting.

In the evening we're going to have dinner at a restaurant near Piazza San Marco with two people from Canada. We met them yesterday on the boat ride from the airport. Their names are Paul and Myra, and they're going to stay in Venice for two weeks.

4. _____

Because it rained all night.

5. _____

On a walking tour of the city.

6. _____

At 9:00.

7. _____

He's sleeping.

8. _____

A professor of art history.

9. _____

At a restaurant near Piazza San Marco.

10. _____

With two people from Canada.

11. _____

Yesterday.

(Continued on next page.)

12. _____

Paul and Myra.

13. _____

For two weeks.

May 22nd

Dinner was great. Paul is a little strange, but I like Myra a lot. Paul and Dan ate too much. Dan was sick all night and didn't fall asleep until five in the morning. It's already 8:30, and he's still sleeping. Dan loves to sleep. (I didn't know that before the wedding. It's okay. I love him anyway!)

---

14. _____

Myra.

15. _____

He ate too much.

16. _____

He loves to sleep.

A.3

How will Carol and Dan's life change after marriage? Complete the sentences. Choose the best answers.

1. Carol and Dan _____ find a place to live.
   a. may
   b. have to

2. Dan _____ go out with other women.
   a. mustn't
   b. doesn't have to

3. Carol and Dan _____ buy a house.
   a. may
   b. must

4. Carol and Dan _____ have a lot of children.
   a. might
   b. have to

5. Carol _____ fight a lot with Dan.
   a. can't
   b. shouldn't

6. Carol and Dan _____ be honest with each other.
   a. can
   b. should

7. Carol and Dan _____ earn money.
   a. may
   b. have to

8. Carol's parents _____ say bad things about Dan.
   a. don't have to
   b. shouldn't

9. Carol and Dan _____ help each other with problems.
   a. ought to
   b. mustn't

10. Carol and Dan _____ listen to Carol's parents.
    a. can't
    b. don't have to

11. Carol _____ be rude to Dan's family.
    a. mustn't
    b. doesn't have to

12. Carol _____ ask permission to get married.
    a. couldn't
    b. didn't have to

B.1

Yoko had teacher A this year and teacher B last year. She liked teacher A more. Here are the reasons. Compare the two teachers. Write sentences.

TEACHER A	**TEACHER B**
1. Teacher A is very patient.	Teacher B isn't very patient.
2. Teacher A is organized.	Teacher B isn't organized.
3. Teacher A is nice.	Teacher B isn't very nice.
4. Teacher A teaches well.	Teacher B doesn't teach well.
5. Teacher A speaks clearly.	Teacher B doesn't speak clearly.
6. Teacher A is friendly.	Teacher B isn't very friendly.
7. Teacher A gives back homework quickly.	Teacher B doesn't give back homework quickly.
8. Teacher A explains things slowly.	Teacher B doesn't explain things slowly.
9. Teacher A gives a little homework.	Teacher B gives a lot of homework.
10. Teacher A rarely makes mistakes.	Teacher B often makes mistakes.
11. Teacher A's class has a relaxed atmosphere.	Teacher B's class doesn't have a relaxed atmosphere.
12. Teacher A gives easy homework.	Teacher B gives difficult homework.
13. Teacher A uses interesting books.	Teacher B doesn't use very interesting books.
14. Teacher A gives long breaks.	Teacher B doesn't give long breaks.
15. Unfortunately, teacher A gives hard tests.	Teacher B doesn't give hard tests.

1. *Teacher A is more patient than teacher B.* _____
2. _____
3. _____
4. _____
5. _____
6. _____
7. _____
8. _____
9. _____
10. _____
11. _____
12. _____
13. _____
14. _____
15. _____

B.2

Rewrite the first eight sentences in exercise B.1. Compare teacher B and teacher A.

1. *Teacher B isn't as patient as teacher A.*

2. _____

3. _____

4. _____

5. _____

6. _____

7. _____

8. _____

B.3

Find the ten differences between the pictures. Write sentences on the next page. Use **a few, a little,** *or* **a lot of.**

(Continued on next page.)

1. *There are a few dishes in the first picture, but there are a lot of dishes in the second picture.*

2. _____

3. _____

4. _____

5. _____

6. _____

7. _____

8. _____

9. _____

10. _____

B.4

Write questions about the first picture on page 223. Use **many** *or* **much** *and the words in the box. Then answer the questions.*

dishes	chairs	flowers	glasses
bread	cheese	fruit	orange juice
butter	chocolate	gifts	potato chips

1. *Are there many dishes?*

   No, there aren't.

2. _____

_____

3. _____

_____

4. _____

_____

5. _____

_____

6. _____

_____

7. _____

_____

8. _____

_____

9. _____

_____

10. _____

_____

11. _____

_____

12. _____

_____

U N I T 8 Simple Past Tense

ANSWER KEY

Where the full form is given, the contraction is also acceptable. Where the contracted form is given, the full form is also acceptable.

A.1

2. i 3. a 4. e 5. g 6. b 7. c 8. f 9. h

A.2

2. Last 3. Last 4. Yesterday 5. yesterday 6. yesterday
7. last

A.3

1. Eric traveled to Poland _____ years ago. 2. Eric visited his college roommate _____ months ago. 3. Eric called his parents _____ days ago. 4. Eric talked to his boss about a raise _____ days ago. 5. Eric graduated from college _____ years ago. 6. Eric moved to Georgia _____ months ago. 7. Eric played tennis _____ days ago. 8. Eric studied Polish _____ years ago. 9. Eric's grandfather died _____ months ago.

A.4

2. They played basketball 3. She washed her clothes
4. They studied 5. He worked in his garden 6. She prepared dinner at 6:00 7. Anna talked to her daughter
8. They traveled to France 9. The bank closed at 3:00 P.M.
10. They watched television

A.5

1. washed; didn't wash 2. invited; didn't invite 3. cleaned; didn't clean 4. talked; didn't talk 5. called; didn't call
6. watched; didn't watch 7. returned; didn't return
8. painted; didn't paint 9. cooked; didn't cook 10. studied; didn't study

A.6

1. am sitting 2. am thinking 3. think 4. is shining 5. are singing 6. rained 7. stayed 8. didn't go 9. washed
10. cleaned 11. played 12. comes 13. speak 14. don't speak 15. laughs 16. invited 17. listened 18. danced
19. enjoyed 20. am cooking 21. need 22. don't want
23. know

B.1

3. *put,* irregular, put 4. *had,* irregular, have 5. *brushed,* regular, brush 6. *left,* irregular, leave 7. *arrived,* regular, arrive 8. *began,* irregular, begin 9. *learned,* regular, learn
10. *finished,* regular, finish 11. *met,* irregular, meet 12. *ate,* irregular, eat 13. *went,* irregular, go 14. *stayed,* regular, stay

B.2

2. drank 3. left 4. met 5. spoke 6. went 7. stole 8. found
9. drove 10. saw 11. brought 12. came

B.3

(Probable answers) 2. I didn't eat three kilos of oranges for breakfast yesterday morning. 3. I didn't sleep twenty-one hours yesterday. 4. I didn't bring a horse to English class two weeks ago. 5. I didn't go to the moon last month. 6. I didn't meet the leader of my country last night. 7. I didn't find $10,000 in a brown paper bag yesterday. 8. I didn't do this exercise two years ago. 9. I didn't swim thirty kilometers yesterday. 10. I didn't speak English perfectly ten years ago.

B.4

1. had 2. didn't get 3. got 4. went 5. met 6. went
7. didn't see 8. didn't have 9. closed 10. ate 11. took
12. stayed 13. looked 14. bought 15. didn't buy 16. came
17. made 18. didn't have 19. drove 20. saw 21. invited
22. didn't eat 23. watched 24. didn't leave

C.1

2. Yes, they did. 3. No, she didn't. 4. Yes, he did. 5. Yes, she did. 6. No, they didn't. 7. No, he didn't. 8. No, they didn't. 9. Yes, he did.

C.2

2. Did you do all the homework? 3. Did you take a bath this morning? 4. Did your best friend come over to your house last night? 5. Did you go to bed early last night? 6. Did your English teacher teach you new grammar last week?
7. Did you visit the United States ten years ago? 8. Did your mother and father get married a long time ago? 9. Did you watch television last night?

C.3

2. Yes, I did. (*or* No, I didn't.) 3. Yes, I did. (*or* No, I didn't.)
4. Yes, he/she did. (*or* No, he/she didn't.) 5. Yes, I did. (*or* No, I didn't.) 6. Yes, he/she did. (*or* No, he/she didn't.)
7. Yes, I did. (*or* No, I didn't.) 8. Yes, they did. (*or* No, they didn't.) 9. Yes, I did. (*or* No, I didn't.)

C.4

3. Did you buy food for dinner? 4. got 5. Did you meet Glen for lunch? 6. ate 7. Did you write a letter to Rena?
8. mailed 9. Did you go to the bank? 10. deposited 11. Did you return the book to the library? 12. took 13. Did you look for a birthday present for Jane? 14. bought 15. Did you call the doctor? 16. said 17. Did you bake some cookies? 18. had 19. Did you pick the children up at 4:00?
20. forgot

D.1

2. k 3. d 4. a 5. i 6. b 7. j 8. g 9. c 10. f

D.2

2. When did a human being walk on the moon for the first time? In 1969. **3.** What did William Shakespeare write? Plays like *Romeo and Juliet*. **4.** Where did the Olympic Games start? In Greece. **5.** Why did many people go to California in 1849? They wanted to find gold. **6.** How long did John Kennedy live in the White House? Almost three years. **7.** What did Alfred Hitchcock make? Movies. **8.** Why did the Chinese build the Great Wall? They wanted to keep foreigners out of the country. **9.** How long did World War II last in Europe? About six years. **10.** When did Christopher Columbus discover America? In 1492.

U N I T ⑨ Simple Past of Be

A.1

3. The shirt was $29.99. **4.** The tie was $16. **5.** The socks were $8. **6.** The sweater was $39. **7.** The coat was $145. **8.** The pajamas were $19.99. **9.** The shirts were $14.99. **10.** The gloves were $25. **11.** The hat was $22. **12.** The shoes were $65.

A.2

3. William Shakespeare and Charles Dickens weren't Canadian. **4.** Ronald Reagan wasn't the first president of the United States. **5.** Charlie Chaplin and Marilyn Monroe were movie stars. **6.** The end of World War I wasn't in 1922. **7.** *E.T.* was the name of a movie. **8.** Toronto and Washington, D.C., weren't big cities 300 years ago. **9.** Indira Gandhi and Napolean were famous people. **10.** Margaret Thatcher was a political leader. **11.** Oregon and Hawaii weren't part of the United States in 1776. **12.** Disneyland wasn't a famous place 100 years ago.

A.3

2. No, they weren't. (*or* Yes, they were.) **3.** Yes, I was. (*or* No, I wasn't.) **4.** Yes, he was. (*or* No, he wasn't.) **5.** Yes, it was. (*or* No, it wasn't.) **6.** Yes, I was. (*or* No, I wasn't.) **9.** Yes, we were. (*or* No, we weren't.) **10.** Yes, I did. (*or* No, I didn't.) **11.** Yes, it was. (*or* No, it wasn't.) **12.** Yes, I did. (*or* No, I didn't.) **13.** Yes, he/she did. (*or* No, he/she didn't.) **14.** Yes I was. (*or* No, I wasn't.) **15.** No, they didn't.

A.4

2. Were they on sale? Yes, they were only $25. **3.** Were you at home last night? No, I was at the library. **4.** Were the guests late for the party? No, they were all on time. **5.** Was it warm in Australia? The weather was beautiful every day. **6.** Was the movie good? It was okay. **7.** Were the people at the party friendly? Most of them were very nice. **8.** Was he there? No, he was at a meeting.

A.5

3. is **4.** is **5.** is **6.** are **7.** is **8.** Is **9.** is **10.** was **11.** was **12.** were **13.** Were **14.** were **15.** were **16.** was **17.** were **18.** were **19.** Are **20.** are

B.1

2. a **3.** a **4.** b **5.** a **6.** a **7.** b **8.** b **9.** b

B.2

1. did **2.** were **3.** did **4.** was **5.** were **6.** did **7.** was **8.** did **9.** was **10.** was **11.** did **12.** were

D.3

2. Who gave **3.** Who did you see **4.** Who called? **5.** Who wrote **6.** Who took **7.** Who did she send **8.** Who cleaned **9.** Who did she marry? **10.** Who did they stay

D.4

2. Who did you go with? (*or* Who went with you?) **3.** What time (*or* When) did you leave your home? **4.** What time (*or* When) did the movie start? **5.** Why did you leave your house so early? **6.** Where did you eat? (*or* Where did you have dinner?) **7.** Where did you meet your friend? **8.** What did you eat (*or* have)? **9.** Who saw you? **10.** Why did you talk to the manager? **11.** Where did you go after dinner? **12.** What did you see? **13.** Where did you see the movie?

B.3

2. How was the weather? **3.** How did you get to the beach? **4.** What was the problem with the bus? **5.** Why did you go there? **6.** Who were you with? **7.** Where did your friends meet you? **8.** Why were your friends late? **9.** What did you wear? **10.** Where was your husband? **11.** Why was he angry? **12.** When did he come home?

B.4

2. were you **3.** was it **4.** were they afraid **5.** was the score **6.** was the name of the store **7.** were they born **8.** were they here **9.** were you with **10.** was Eleanor Roosevelt **11.** were your teachers

C.1

✔ - 1, 3, 6, 7, 9

C.2

1. There was **2.** There were **3.** There was **4.** There was **5.** There were **6.** There were **7.** There was **8.** There were **9.** There were **10.** There was

C.3

2. There was, There weren't **3.** There was, There were **4.** There was, There were **5.** There weren't, There was **6.** There was, There were **7.** There was, There weren't **8.** There weren't, There was

C.4

1. Yes, there was. (*or* No, there wasn't.) **2.** Yes, there were. (*or* No, there weren't.) **3.** Yes, there was. (*or* No, there wasn't.) **4.** Yes, there was. (*or* No, there wasn't.) **5.** Yes, there were. (*or* No, there weren't.) **6.** Yes, there were. (*or* No, there weren't.) **7.** Yes, there was. (*or* No, there wasn't.) **8.** Yes, there were. (*or* No, there weren't.)

C.5

2. Was there a view of the sea from your hotel room? **3.** Was there a restaurant in the hotel? **4.** Was there a beach near the hotel? **5.** Were there cheap restaurants? **6.** Were there interesting things to see? **7.** Were there many places to go shopping? **8.** Were there many English-speaking people? **9.** Was there a casino on the island?

U N I T 10 Nouns and Quantifiers; Modals: <u>Can, Could, Would</u>

A.1

2. 5 **3.** 7 **4.** 1 **5.** 9 **6.** 8 **7.** 4 **8.** 1 **9.** 8 **10.** 4 **11.** 5 **12.** 7 **13.** 2 **14.** 8 **15.** 3

A.2

Count Nouns — eggs, vegetables, napkins, bags, potato chips, toothbrushes

Non-count Nouns — ice cream, fruit, milk, rice, food, bread, fish

A.3

Count Nouns — a student, some teeth, some children, some friends, an animal, some people, an uncle, a television, some questions, a computer

Non-count Nouns — some water, some paper, some homework, some advice, some traffic, some furniture, some money, some information, some rain, some oil

A.4

2. a **3.** a **4.** b **5.** a **6.** a **7.** a **8.** b **9.** a **10.** a **11.** b

A.5

3. He bought some orange juice. **4.** He didn't buy any lemons. **5.** He bought a newspaper. **6.** He didn't buy any bread. **7.** He didn't buy any onions. **8.** He didn't buy a toothbrush. **9.** He bought some potatoes. **10.** He didn't buy any lettuce. **11.** He didn't buy any carrots. **12.** He bought some butter. **13.** He bought some milk. **14.** He bought some eggs.

A.6

a lot of/any — food in my refrigerator, money in my pocket, books next to my bed, shirts in my closet, friends, free time, children, work to do today, questions for my teacher, jewelry, medicine in my bathroom, problems with English grammar, photographs in my wallet, ice cream at home

a little/much — cheese in my pocket, food in my refrigerator, money in my pocket, free time, work to do today, jewelry, medicine in my bathroom, ice cream at home

a few/many — books next to my bed, shirts in my closet, friends, children, questions for my teacher, problems with English grammar, photographs in my wallets

B.1

2. d **3.** a **4.** c **5.** g **6.** h **7.** f **8.** e **9.** l **10.** k **11.** j **12.** i

B.2

3. One carton. **4.** Two heads. **5.** Three. **6.** One. **7.** Four rolls. **8.** Three bars. **9.** One tube. **10.** Two.

B.3

4. Is there any furniture in your home? **5.** Are there any clothes in your closet? **6.** Is there any money under your bed? **7.** Is there an alarm clock next to your bed? **8.** Is there any snow on the ground outside your home? **9.** Is there a sink in your bathroom? **10.** Are there any dishes in your kitchen sink? **11.** Are there any pictures on the walls of your bedroom? **12.** Is there any candy in your home? **13.** Is there a window in your kitchen? **14.** Is there a television in your living room?

B.4

1. Yes, there is. (*or* No, there isn't.) **2.** Yes, there are. (*or* No, there aren't.) **3.** Yes, there is. (*or* No, there isn't.) **4.** Yes, there is. (*or* No, there isn't.) **5.** Yes, there are. (*or* No, there aren't.) **6.** Yes, there is. (*or* No, there isn't.) **7.** Yes, there is. (*or* No, there isn't.) **8.** Yes, there is. (*or* No, there isn't.) **9.** Yes, there is. (*or* No, there isn't.) **10.** Yes, there are. (*or* No, there aren't.) **11.** Yes, there are. (*or* No, there aren't.) **12.** Yes, there is. (*or* No, there isn't.) **13.** Yes, there is. (*or* No, there isn't.) **14.** Yes, there is. (*or* No, there isn't.)

B.5

3. How much flour do you need? **4.** How much sugar do you have? **5.** How many bananas do you want? **6.** How many oranges do you want? **7.** How much rice do you need? **8.** How many potatoes do you need? **9.** How much milk do you want? **10.** How many roses do you want? **11.** How many cookies do you have? **12.** How much money do you have?

C.1

2. b **3.** a **4.** b **5.** a **6.** b **7.** b **8.** a **9.** b **10.** a

C.2

2. There are too many days. **3.** There are too many numbers. **4.** There is too much water. **5.** There is too much furniture. **6.** There is too much food. **7.** There are too many birds. **8.** There too much shampoo. **9.** There are not enough batteries. **10.** There is not enough toothpaste. **11.** There is not enough air. **12.** There are not enough chairs.

C.3

3. There were too few people for two teams. **4.** We had too little paper for everyone in the class. **5.** There was too little food for fifteen people. **6.** You have too little information. **7.** There are too many bedrooms in that apartment. **8.** We had too little time for that test. **9.** There are too few bananas for a banana cake. **10.** There are too few sales people at that store.

D.1

2. secretary **3.** driver **4.** summer camp worker

D.2

4. He can drive, and lift 100 pounds. **5.** He can type, and speak Spanish. **6.** She can play the guitar, and draw. **7.** He can't drive, and he can't lift 100 pounds. **8.** She can type, but she can't speak Spanish. **9.** She can lift 100 pounds, but she can't drive. **10.** He can draw, but he can't play the guitar. **11.** She can't draw, and she can't play the guitar. **12.** He can't type, and he can't speak Spanish.

D.3

2. Can your mother lift 100 pounds? 3. Can your father play the guitar? 4. Can your best friend ride a horse? 5. Can your parents speak Spanish? 6. Can you swim? 7. Can you type?

D.4

1. Yes, I can. (*or* No, I can't.) 2. Yes, she can. (*or* No, she can't.) 3. Yes, he can. (*or* No, he can't.) 4. Yes, he/she can. (*or* No, he/she can't.) 5. Yes, they can. (*or* No, they can't.) 6. Yes, I can. (*or* No, I can't.) 7. Yes, I can. (*or* No, I can't.)

D.5

2. could practice 3. couldn't go 4. couldn't understand 5. couldn't eat 6. could play 7. couldn't find 8. could hear 9. couldn't use 10. could do

D.6

2. Can I (*or* May I) open the window? 3. Can I (*or* May I) use the telephone? 4. Can I (*or* May I) give you a ride? 5. Can I (*or* May I) use (*or* borrow) your eraser? 6. Can I (*or* May I) have a drink of water? 7. Can I (*or* May I) ask you a question? 8. Can I (*or* May I) sit at the empty table in the corner?

E.1

1. At the bus station 2. On an airplane 3. At a movie theater

E.2

2. Would you like to have dinner with me? 3. Sheila would like to talk to you. 4. Would your parents like to come?

5. Sandy and Billy would like some coffee. 6. Would Dan like to come with us? 7. My friend and I would like a table for two. 8. Would the teacher like to come to the party? 9. I would like to take a long trip. 10. We would like you to have dinner with us.

E.3

2. Ari would like Conchita to bring the CDs. 3. Ari would like Irene and Amira to help with the cooking. 4. Ari would like Eric to bring his CD player. 5. Ari would like Harry, Mike, and Tom to move the furniture. 6. Ari would like Ellen to buy some ice cream. 7. Ari would like Victor to pick up the birthday cake. 8. Ari would like Carmen and Ted to keep Tony busy. 9. Ari would like Ratana to make the decorations.

E.4

2. Would you like 3. Would you like 4. would like 5. Would you like me to give 6. What would you like to do 7. Where would you like to go 8. Would you like to go 9. Would you like to see 10. What time would you like to go 11. would like to get 12. Where would you like to eat

E.5

2. Would (*or* Could) you please give me the key to my room? 3. Would (*or* Could) you please explain the meaning of the word *grateful*? 4. Would (*or* Could) you please give me change for a dollar? 5. Would (*or* Could) you please take a picture of me and my friends? 6. Would (*or* Could) you please take me to the airport? 7. Would (*or* Could) you please help me with my suitcases 8. Would (*or* Could) you please show me the brown shoes in the window? Would (*or* Could) you please sit down?

UNIT 11 Future; Modals: Ｍａy and Ｍ_i_ght

A.1

2. this evening 3. next month 4. tomorrow morning 5. next week 6. tonight 7. tomorrow night

A.2

2. in two weeks 3. in three days 4. in two months 5. in ten minutes

A.3

Answers will vary.

A.4

(Possible answers) I am (*or* am not) going to study. I am (*or* am not) going to go shopping. I am (*or* am not) going to clean. I am (*or* am not) going to watch TV. I am (*or* am not) going to go out with friends. I am (*or* am not) going to listen to music. I am (*or* am not) going to visit relatives. I am (*or* am not) going to talk on the telephone. I am (*or* am not) going to take a shower. I am (*or* am not) going to write a letter. I am (*or* am not) going to read a newspaper. I am (*or* am not) going to stay home.

A.5

2. She's going to play tennis. 3. She's going to swim. 4. They're going to fish. 5. They're going to ride bikes.

6. They're going to write letters. 7. He's going to take pictures. 8. He's going to ski. 9. He's going to read. 10. He's going to play the guitar.

A.6

2. She isn't going to take 3. She isn't going to take 4. They aren't going to play 5. They aren't going to watch 6. I'm not going to have 7. We're not going to go 8. He isn't going to see 9. I'm not going to wake up 10. He isn't going to deliver

A.7

2. Who is going to cook tonight? 3. When is dinner going to be ready? 4. Why is he going to cook so much food? 5. How long is he going to need to cook the dinner? 6. Who is going to come? 7. How is he going to cook the lamb? 8. Where are all of your guests going to sit? 9. What are you going to do? 10. How long are your guests going to stay?

A.8

2. What's he going to make? 3. Why's he going to cook so much food? 4. How's he going to cook the lamb? 5. Who's going to come? 6. How long's he going to need to cook the dinner? 7. What're you going to do? 8. When's dinner going to be ready? 9. How long are your guests going to stay? 10. Where're all of your guests going to sit?

B.1

3. <u>am doing</u>, now 4. <u>are going</u>, future 5. <u>is leaving</u>, future
6. <u>Are . . . doing</u>, now 7. <u>Is . . . coming</u>, future 8. <u>are . . .
listening</u>, now 9. <u>are . . . going</u>, now 10. <u>is . . . going</u>, now

B.2

2. They are flying to London at 7:30 on May 8. 3. They are
arriving in London at 6:45 A.M. on May 9. 4. They are staying
at the London Regency Hotel on May 9 and 10. 5. They are
visiting Buckingham Palace at 2 P.M. on May 9. 6. They are
having tea at the Ritz Hotel at 4:30 on May 9. 7. They are
going to the theater at 7:30 on May 9. 8. They are going on a
tour of central London at 9:00 A.M. on May 10. 9. They are eating lunch at a typical English pub at twelve o'clock on May 10.
10. They are leaving for Scotland at 8:00 A.M. on May 11.

B.3

2. Are you going to the movies this weekend? 3. Are you taking a trip next week? 4. Is your friend coming over to your
place in two hours? 5. Are your classmates from English
class meeting you for lunch tomorrow afternoon? 6. Is your
mother driving to work tomorrow? 7. Is your father taking
an English class next year? 8. Are your neighbors making a
party for you this weekend? 9. Are you and your friends
playing cards next Saturday? 10. Are your parents having
dinner with your English teacher the day after tomorrow?

B.4

1. Yes, I am. (or No, I'm not.) 2. Yes, I am. (or No, I'm not.)
3. Yes, I am. (or No, I'm not.) 4. Yes, he/she is. (or No,
he/she isn't.) 5. Yes, they are. (or No, they aren't.) 6. Yes,
she is. (or No, she isn't.) 7. Yes, he is. (or No, he isn't.)
8. Yes, they are. (or No, they aren't.) 9. Yes, we are. (or No,
we aren't.) 10. Yes, they are. (or No, they aren't.)

B.5

2. When are you leaving? 3. How are you getting there? (or
How are you going?) 4. Why are you driving? 5. How long
are you staying? 6. Who are you going with? 7. What are
you taking?

C.1

2. I'll get you some water. 3. I'll help you. 4. I'll buy you
some. 5. I'll turn on the air conditioner. 6. I'll make you a
sandwich. 7. I'll get you some aspirin. 8. I'll drive you.
9. I'll wash them.

C.2

2. It will be sunny tomorrow. 3. They will not know the
story. 4. It will not be easy. 5. We will take you to Ottawa.

U N I T 12 Comparisons

A.1

✓-2, 3, 5, 7

A.2

one syllable — fast, high, hot, long, old, small

two syllables — crowded, easy, friendly, heavy, messy,
noisy, pretty

6. I will not stay there for a long time. 7. He will tell you
later.

C.3

2. He won't lose his job. 3. I'll have a cup of coffee. 4. It'll
rain this evening. 5. She won't be happy. 6. They'll have a
good time. 7. You won't like it.

C.4

2. a 3. b 4. a 5. a 6. b 7. b 8. a 9. b

C.5

2. I won't leave late. 3. It won't be hot. 4. Coffee won't cost
more. 5. The dishes won't be dirty. 6. We won't come
before seven o'clock. 7. Mr. and Mrs. McNamara won't buy
a new car. 8. I won't make many eggs. 9. Valeria won't lose
the game. 10. The parking lot won't be full.

C.6

1. will be 2. Will I be 3. will marry 4. will I meet 5. will be
6. Will she love 7. will we meet 8. won't have 9. will be
10. will I be 11. won't be 12. will bother 13. won't like
14. Will our home have 15. won't leave 16. won't bother
17. will become 18. Will that make

D.1

3. permission 4. possibility 5. possibility 6. permission
7. possibility 8. permission 9. possibility 10. permission

D.2

2. We may (or might) come by taxi. 3. He may (or might)
not want to come. 4. They may (or might) study. 5. The
store may (or might) be closed. 6. She may (or might) not
finish the work by Friday. 7. The dog may (or might) die.
8. You may (or might) not like that kind of food. 9. I may
(or might) not leave before seven o'clock. 10. The cookies
may (or might) not taste good.

D.3

3. may 4. will 5. will 6. may 7. may 8. will 9. will 10. may

D.4

2. may (or might) not pass 3. may (or might) have an
accident 4. may (or might) break 5. may (or might) not
win 6. may (or might) get lost 7. may (or might) not live
8. may (or might) bite 9. may (or might) get sick 10. may
(or might) close

three or four syllables — dangerous, difficult, expensive,
intelligent

A.3

2. better 3. farther 4. more intelligent 5. worse 6. messier
7. more comfortable 8. more careful 9. prettier 10. more
difficult 11. easier

A.4

2. longer than 3. more expensive than 4. bigger than
5. higher than 6. hotter than 7. more dangerous than
8. more crowded than 9. noisier than 10. heavier than
11. faster than 12. friendlier than

A.5

1. Is this unit easier or more difficult than the last unit?
2. Is this workbook cheaper or more expensive than the
grammar book? 3. Are you younger or older than your best
friend? 4. Are you taller or shorter than your teacher? 5. Is
your hometown bigger or smaller than Los Angeles? 6. Is
the weather today better or worse than the weather
yesterday?

A.6

1. It is more difficult. (*or* It is easier.) 2. It is cheaper. 3. I am
younger (*or* I am older.) 4. I am taller. (*or* I am shorter.) 5. It
is smaller. (*or* It is bigger.) 6. It is better. (*or* It is worse.)

B.1

3. adverb 4. adjective 5. adverb 6. adverb 7. adverb
8. adjective 9. adjective 10. adverb 11. adverb
12. adjective

B.2

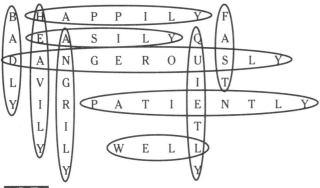

B.3

2. quietly 3. dangerously 4. angrily 5. happily 6. well
7. badly 8. fast 9. patiently 10. easily

B.4

2. beautiful, beautiful 3. fast, fast 4. tired, tired 5. well,
good 6. carefully, careful 7. loud, loudly (*or* loud) 8. angrily, angry 9. easy, easily

B.5

2. harder 3. better 4. more carefully 5. faster 6. more neatly
7. worse 8. more quickly 9. more easily 10. higher 11. more
rudely

C.1

2. f 3. h 4. c 5. a 6. d 7. e 8. g

C.2

2. The apartment is too small for six people. 3. Shirley and
Jack are too slow to run in the race. 4. The car is too
expensive for us to buy. 5. The children are too young to
start school. 6. The room is too cold.

C.3

2. The jacket isn't big enough for me. 3. The break wasn't
long enough. 4. It isn't light enough to take a picture. 5. It
isn't quiet enough to talk. 6. Buses aren't fast enough.

C.4

1. very 2. too 3. too 4. very 5. very 6. too 7. very
8. very 9. too

C.5

2. This coffee is too strong for me to drink. 3. The
instructions were too difficult for Pete to understand.
4. The fruit is not ripe enough for us to eat. 5. The line is
too long for us to wait. 6. The sweater was too dirty for her
to wash by hand. 7. He is not rich enough for you to marry.
8. The eggs are cooked enough for you to eat.

C.6

3. too frightened 4. not big enough 5. too late 6. hot
enough 7. too tight 8. too short 9. not safe enough
10. warm enough 11. not sunny enough

D.1

✓-2, 3, 4, 6, 7

D.2

3. as 4. than 5. as 6. than 7. as 8. as 9. as 10. than
11. than 12. than

D.3

4. Trains aren't as fast as airplanes. 5. January is as cold as
February. 6. The chair is as comfortable as the sofa.
7. The governor of Oregon isn't as famous as the president
of the United States. 8. The bank isn't as far as the post
office. 9. Grapefruits are as sour as lemons. 10. Jazz is
more relaxing than rock music. 11. Chocolate ice cream
isn't as good as vanilla ice cream. 12. Some people are
more violent than other people. 13. College isn't as easy as
high school. 14. These boxes are as heavy as those boxes.

D.4

2. Are you the same height as your brother? 3. Is your
mother the same age as your father? 4. Is the dining room
the same size as the living room? 5. Are the apples the
same price as the oranges? 6. Are you the same weight as
your brother? 7. Is *War and Peace* the same length as
Crime and Punishment? 8. Is the subway station the same
distance as the bus stop?

D.5

3. A bike is the same as a bicycle. 4. A TV is the same as a
television. 5. North America is different from the United
States. 6. 10,362 is different from 10.362. 7. 3 x 16 is the
same as 16 x 3. 8. 16 ÷ 3 is different from 3 ÷ 16. 9. $1 is
different from £1. 10. A snack bar is different from a
restaurant. 11. 12:00 P.M. is the same as noon. 12. A plane
is the same as an airplane.

E.1

1. a 2. b 3. b 4. a 5. b 6. b 7. b 8. b

F13

E.2

fewer—brothers, cars, children, courses, friends, hours, mistakes, pairs of shoes, women

less—coffee, food, free time, fruit, furniture, homework, meat, money, traffic

E.3

4. has more brothers than Noah **5.** works fewer hours a week than Noah **6.** makes less money an hour than Noah **7.** is taking more courses this semester than Noah **8.** drinks fewer cups of coffee (or less coffee) a day than Noah **9.** has more bedrooms than Noah's house **10.** has less free time than Noah **11.** has fewer pairs of shoes than Noah **12.** eats less meat than Noah **13.** has more cars than Noah's family **14.** has more children than Noah's brother **15.** made fewer mistakes on last week's test than Noah

UNIT 13 Past Progressive; Direct and Indirect Objects

A.1

Answers will vary.

A.2

2. She was talking on the phone. **3.** They were waiting in line. **4.** They were studying. **5.** She was typing. **6.** He was buying some groceries. **7.** She was taking a shower. **8.** She was cooking dinner. **9.** He was getting gas. **10.** He was going to school.

A.3

3. wasn't reading **4.** were waiting **5.** weren't standing **6.** was wearing **7.** wasn't holding **8.** wasn't buying **9.** weren't leaving

A.4

2. While my father was talking to me, someone rang the doorbell. **3.** The boys were playing basketball when the fight started. **4.** I was swimming when I got a pain in the leg. **5.** When we saw the accident, we were driving down Market Street. **6.** The doctor was examining Mrs. May when she screamed. **7.** While I was washing my hair, I got some soap in my eyes. **8.** Alan was shaving when he cut himself. **9.** The train came while we were getting our tickets.

A.5

2. Was he meeting with his salespeople **3.** Was she teaching **4.** Was he swimming **5.** Was she practicing the piano **6.** Was he listening to a business report on the radio **7.** Were they having dinner **8.** Were they watching the news **9.** Was she taking a bath

A.6

1a. were having **1b.** hurried **2a.** was watching **2b.** answered **3a.** were sleeping **3b.** ran **4a.** were standing **4b.** sat **5a.** was climbing **5b.** called **6a.** was ironing **6b.** put

A.7

2. What were you doing? **3.** What were you waiting for? **4.** Where were you going? **5.** Why were you going to the gym? **6.** Who was driving **7.** How fast was he going (or driving)? **8.** Why was he driving (or going) so fast? **9.** Who was riding

B.1

2. e **3.** g **4.** b **5.** c **6.** h **7.** i **8.** d **9.** a

E.4

2. Joanne is a better student than Steve and Harry. **3.** Mr. Page makes more serious mistakes than the other two salesmen. **4.** This is a more difficult book than the other ones. **5.** The apartment on the second floor has a bigger kitchen than the apartments on the first floor. **6.** Police officers have more dangerous jobs than secretaries. **7.** India has a bigger population than Spain.

E.5

2. A big city usually has more crowded streets than a small town. **3.** A big city usually has a more exciting night life than a small town. **4.** A small town usually has friendlier people than a big city. **5.** A big city usually has a larger police department than a small town. **6.** A big city usually has more serious parking problems than a small town. **7.** A small town usually has a slower way of life than a big city. **8.** A small town usually has a smaller public transportation system than a big city.

B.2

2. answers, you **3.** this check, me **4.** the car, you **5.** the salt and pepper, me **6.** my car, you **7.** something, my mother **8.** the information, you **9.** your passport, me

B.3

2. Kate got a silver bowl for Stephen and Margo. **3.** Tim and June bought a TV for Stephen and Margo. **4.** Julie sent a painting to Stephen and Margo. **5.** Mike and Sally gave some dishes to Stephen and Margo. **6.** Robert made the wedding cake for Stephen and Margo.

B.4

2. He's going to give Bob a CD. **3.** He's going to give Bill a book. **4.** He's going to give Marge some earrings. **5.** He's going to give his brother some pajamas. **6.** He's going to give his cousin some sunglasses.

B.5

2. it to them **3.** them to her **4.** them to me **5.** them for her **6.** it for them **7.** them for me **8.** it to me **9.** it for him **10.** it to them

B.6

5. I lent some money to him. **3.** Would you pronounce this for me? **4.** The man is showing something to the women. **5.** Can you give them some help? **6.** Did you tell him the answer? **7.** I got these cookies for the children **8.** I send all my friends birthday cards. **9.** Sharon fixed my watch for me. **10.** Throw the ball to me. **11.** Would you explain this sentence to us? **12.** He owes me fifty dollars.

C.1

2. too **3.** too **4.** too **5.** either **6.** either **7.** too **8.** either **9.** either

C.2

2. is **3.** didn't **4.** does **5.** does **6.** wasn't **7.** doesn't **8.** doesn't **9.** isn't **10.** did **11.** can **12.** won't

C.3

3. and her father does, too **4.** and her brother did, too **5.** and her sister isn't, either. **6.** and her father didn't, either **7.** and her brother was, too **8.** and her sister is, too **9.** and her sister wasn't, either **10.** and her father does, too **11.** and her mother can't, either **12.** and her mother doesn't, either

D.1

2. on 3. on 4. off 5. in 6. off 7. away 8. away 9. away
10. back

D.2

2. I'll put the food away. I'll put it away. 3. I'll turn the radio down. I'll turn it down. 4. Let's put the meeting off. Let's put it off. 5. Please hand these papers out. Please hand them out. 6. I threw the wrong thing away. I threw it away.
7. Please take your shoes off. Please take them off. 8. The store will not take bathing suits back. The store will not take them back. 9. Turn the engine off. Turn it off.
10. Don't put any makeup on. Don't put it on.

D.3

2. turn it on 3. turn it off 4. throw it away 5. give it back
6. put them on 7. turn it up 8. put them away 9. look it up
10. call them up

E.1

2. We like to eat out. 3. The weather will clear up. 4. Some cars often break down. 5. The taxi will show up soon.
6. Don't hang up. 7. Short skirts will probably catch on again.

E.2

2. Put it on. 3. no change 4. no change 5. Throw it away.
6. no change 7. no change 8. Could you turn it off? 9. no change 10. It didn't work right, so I took it back.

E.3

2. hung up 3. cleared up 4. grew up 5. sat down 6. broke down 7. showed up 8. came up 9. ate out 10. shut up
11. stayed up 12. woke up

UNIT 14 Modals: Should, Had better, Have to, Must; Superlatives

A.1

2. shouldn't 3. should 4. shouldn't 5. shouldn't 6. should
7. should 8. shouldn't 9. should 10. shouldn't

A.2

2. I ought to visit my grandparents more often. 3. All passengers ought to arrive at the airport an hour before their flight. 4. Carol ought to study harder. 5. We ought to take something to the party.

A.3

2. You should cook the meat a little longer. 3. Lulu should be nicer to Elenore. 4. I should learn how to type. 5. Pete and Elenore should move into a smaller apartment.

A.4

2. should look for another one. 3. shouldn't smoke.
4. should go to the dentist. 5. should wash it. 6. shouldn't leave a tip. 7. should study more. 8. should leave early.
9. shouldn't watch it. 10. shouldn't touch it.

A.5

2. Why should we have 3. How many (or How many people) should we invite? 4. Who should we invite? 5. What should we buy? 6. What should we cook? 7. Where should we get
8. What should we do? 9. When should we send

B.1

a. — We'd better ask for directions. We'd better look at a map.

b. — We'd better not stay in the sun anymore. We'd better put some cream on our arms and legs.

c. — We'd better not wait for the bus.

d. — We'd better make sure everything is locked. We'd better throw away the food in the refrigerator.

e. — We'd better not stay up late. We'd better get a good night's sleep.

B.2

2. had better not sit together at the table. 3. had better invite him. 4. had better not serve shrimp. 5. had better get a couple of bottles. 6. had better not let the dog in the house.

7. had better borrow some from the neighbors. 8. had better rent a video film. 9. had better ask Costas to bring her.

C.1

Answers will vary.

C.2

2. don't have to do the last exercise again. 3. didn't have to go to school yesterday. 4. had to clean her room yesterday.
5. doesn't have to write her parents every week. 6. didn't have to go shopping last week. 7. have to take tests.
8. don't have to buy a new car. 9. has to see her doctor today. 10. have to check my answers to this exercise.

C.3

2. have to; don't have to 3. don't have to; have to 4. have to; don't have to 5. don't have to; have to 6. have to; don't have to 7. don't have to; have to 8. have to; don't have to
9. have to; don't have to 10. don't have to; have to

C.4

2. has to leave early today. 3. have to go food shopping today.
4. have to come by taxi. 5. doesn't have to stay at the office late today. 6. don't have to clean up their room. 7. has to take some medicine. 8. don't have to pay for the tickets. 9. has to wear a suit and tie this morning. 10. doesn't have to do housework.

C.5

2. You must stop. 3. You mustn't turn right. 4. You mustn't turn left. 5. You mustn't drive faster than 55 mph.
6. You mustn't park in this area. 7. You mustn't make a U-turn. 8. You mustn't pass. 9. You must go more slowly.

C.6

2. They had to find someone to take care of their dog. 3. They had to get to the airport on time. 4. They didn't have to get up early every morning. 5. They didn't have to go to work. 6. They had to look for a hotel. 7. They didn't have to make the bed every morning. 8. They had to pack and unpack suitcases. 9. They had to pay their hotel bill. 10. They didn't have to wash dishes.

C.7

2. Does your mother have to get up at 6:00 in the morning?
3. Did you have to cook last night? 4. Does your best friend

have to do this exercise? **5.** Do you have to be in English class on time? **6.** Do your friends have to learn English? **7.** Did your father have to shave yesterday? **8.** Did your best friend have to go to work yesterday? **9.** Did you have to take a test last week?

C.8

2. Yes, she does. (*or* No, she doesn't.) **3.** Yes, I did. (*or* No, I didn't.) **4.** Yes, he/she does. (*or* No, he/she doesn't.) **5.** Yes, I do. (*or* No, I don't.) **6.** Yes, they do. (*or* No, they don't.) **7.** Yes, he did. (*or* No, he didn't.) **8.** Yes, he/she did. (*or* No, he/she didn't.) **9.** Yes, I did. (*or* No, I didn't.)

C.9

2. does she have to get a book from the library? **3.** does he have to go? **4.** did the teacher have to talk to? **5.** did you have to stay there? **6.** do the students have to stay after class? **7.** do you have to use? **8.** did the high school students have to send their college applications? **9.** do you have to get up? **10.** did he have to borrow?

D.1

2. Doug **3.** Norma **4.** Carol **5.** Norma **6.** Carol **7.** Doug

D.2

2. the worst **3.** the hardest **4.** the most beautiful **5.** the

Putting It All Together

A.1

2. We are having a wonderful time on our honeymoon. **3.** . . . Venice is such a romantic place. **4.** It has so many beautiful places. **5.** Yesterday we walked all around the city. **6.** We visited several churches. **7.** They were so wonderful . . . **8.** . . . we saw so many gorgeous paintings. **9.** . . . we didn't go far from our hotel. **10.** This afternoon we had lunch . . . **11.** We both ate special Venetian dishes . . . **12.** . . . Dan is resting **13.** . . . we are going to take a gondola ride.

A.2

2. Where is their hotel? **3.** What are they going to do tonight? **4.** Why did they stay in their hotel last night? **5.** Where are they going today? **6.** What time will the tour start? **7.** What is Dan doing? **8.** Who is the tour guide? **9.** Where are they going to have dinner (in the evening)? **10.** Who are they going to have dinner with? **11.** When did Carol and Dan meet two people from Canada? **12.** What are the two people's names? **13.** How long are Paul and Myra going to stay in Venice? **14.** Who does Carol like a lot? **15.** Why was Dan sick all night? **16.** What does Dan love to do?

A.3

1. b **2.** a **3.** a **4.** a **5.** b **6.** b **7.** b **8.** b **9.** a **10.** b **11.** a **12.** b

B.1

2. Teacher A is more organized than teacher B. **3.** Teacher A is nicer than teacher B. **4.** Teacher A teaches better than teacher B. **5.** Teacher A speaks more clearly than teacher B. **6.** Teacher A is friendlier than teacher B. **7.** Teacher A gives back homework more quickly than teacher B. **8.** Teacher A explains things more slowly than teacher B. **9.** Teacher A gives less homework than teacher B. **10.** Teacher A makes fewer mistakes than teacher B. **11.** Teacher A's class has a more relaxed atmosphere than teacher B's class. **12.** Teacher A gives easier homework than teacher B. **13.** Teacher A uses more interesting books than teacher B. **14.** Teacher A gives

busiest **6.** the funniest **7.** the best **8.** the ugliest **9.** the most popular **10.** the lowest **11.** the fastest **12.** the most charming

D.3

2. A teenager is the oldest of the three. A child is older than a baby. **3.** A Rolls Royce is the most expensive of the three. A BMW is more expensive than a Ford. **4.** Nigeria is the hottest of the three. Turkey is hotter than Sweden. **5.** A highway is the widest of the three. A street is wider than a path. **6.** A city is the biggest of the three. A town is bigger than a village. **7.** An elephant is the heaviest of the three. A gorilla is heavier than a fox. **8.** An hour is the longest of the three. A minute is longer than a second. **9.** Boxing is the most dangerous of the three. Soccer is more dangerous than golf. **10.** Chocolate is the most fattening of the three. A banana is more fattening than a carrot.

D.4

1. Andy came the earliest. **2.** The red car is going the most slowly (*or* slowest). The white car is going the fastest. **3.** Fran drives the most dangerously. Shirley drives the most carefully. **4.** Gary works the closest to his home. Harris works the farthest from his home. **5.** Carolyn speaks Spanish the best. Milton speaks Spanish the worst. **6.** Renée types the most quickly. Joan types the most accurately.

longer breaks than teacher B. **15.** Unfortunately, Teacher A gives harder tests than teacher B.

B.2

2. Teacher B isn't as organized as teacher A. **3.** Teacher B isn't as nice as teacher A. **4.** Teacher B doesn't teach as well as teacher A. **5.** Teacher B doesn't speak as clearly as teacher A. **6.** Teacher B isn't as friendly as teacher A. **7.** Teacher B doesn't give back homework as quickly as teacher A. **8.** Teacher B doesn't explain things as slowly as teacher A.

B.3

2. There are a few glasses in the first picture, but there are a lot of glasses in the second picture. **3.** There are a lot of flowers in the first picture, but there are a few flowers in the second picture. **4.** There is a lot of Coke in the first picture, but there is a little Coke in the second picture. **5.** There is a little chocolate in the first picture, but there is a lot of chocolate in the second picture. **6.** There are a few candles on the cake in the first picture, but there are a lot of candles on the cake in the second picture. **7.** There is a lot of fruit in the first picture, but there is a little fruit in the second picture. **8.** There is a lot of cheese in the first picture, but there is a little cheese in the second picture. **9.** There is a little bread in the first picture, but there is a lot of bread in the second picture. **10.** There are a few gifts in the first picture, but there are a lot of gifts in the second picture.

B.4

2. Is there much bread? No, there isn't. **3.** Is there much butter? No, there isn't. **4.** Are there many chairs? Yes, there are. **5.** Is there much cheese? Yes, there is. **6.** Is there much chocolate? No, there isn't. **7.** Are there many flowers? Yes, there are. **8.** Is there much fruit? Yes, there is. **9.** Are there many gifts? No, there aren't. **10.** Are there many glasses? No, there aren't. **11.** Is there much orange juice? Yes, there is. **12.** Are there many potato chips? Yes, there are.